DEMOCRACY RENEWED

Andrew Rowe was born in London and educated at Eton (where he was subsequently a master) and at Merton College, Oxford, where he read history. He worked in the Scottish Office where he helped to prepare the reorganization of social work in Scotland and then became a lecturer in Social Administration at Edinburgh University. He has been chairman of the education and training working party of the Scottish Standing Conference of Social Work Organizations and is currently a member of the executive committees of the Scottish Council of Social Service and of the Social Administration Association. He has spent the last year as consultant to the Voluntary Services Unit of the Home Office. Andrew Rowe has contributed articles to such journals as *New Society, Social Work Today, Health and Social Services Journal, The Times Higher Education Supplement* and *The Scotsman* and is the author of booklets about social work organization and community councils.

Publishers' Note

Andrew Rowe is Consultant to the Voluntary Services Unit of the Home Office and not, as stated on the cover, adviser to the Lord Privy Seal's Office. The publishers regret that the covers had already been printed when this error was brought to their notice and apologize for any confusion it may cause.

DEMOCRACY RENEWED
The Community Council in Practice

ANDREW ROWE

SHELDON PRESS
LONDON

First published in Great Britain in 1975 by
Sheldon Press
Marylebone Road, London NW1 4DU

Printed in Great Britain by Northumberland Press Limited,
Gateshead

ISBN 0 85969 038 5 cased
ISBN 0 85969 039 3 paper

For Jill

Contents

Acknowledgements

My debts are legion, whether for practical help, like the loan of a quiet cottage at a critical moment, or for facts and figures culled from helpful and kind civil servants who prefer to remain anonymous. Most of all, perhaps, for typing. Although it is invidious to single out individuals when I owe so much, it would be wrong not to thank very much Miss Watson, Mrs Scott and Mrs Livingstone for their endless help and for their skilful typing, often at time of great stress. I have picked so many people's brains that I ought to make an enormous list of them, but since I take full responsibility for how the ideas have come out in the book, perhaps it is best to leave them unacknowledged. They will know who they are.

I am truly grateful.

Introduction

This book was written at a time when the British people were finding it unusually difficult to believe that they had adequate machinery available to them for solving the country's problems. Wherever they looked they saw new evidence that the pessimism of those commentators who, over the previous decade, had suggested that existing political processes were insufficient to cope with the problems facing Britain at the end of the twentieth century, were right. At a time when inflation appeared to have the whole of the non-totalitarian world in its grasp and our dependence upon politically unstable, largely hostile foreign states had been shown to be almost total, the British endured an unwanted election notable for the almost complete absence of either hope or idealism and voted for a House of Commons incapable of forming a majority government.

For over a decade the British had listened to politicians alternately telling them they were better off than ever before and that by the end of the century they would be the poorest country in Europe. They were confused by hearing that great strides had been made towards an equal society while strident and seemingly well founded arguments revealed that the poor were relatively poorer than ever. They had seen huge efforts made to improve management techniques whether in business, the civil service or the House of Commons but had been stunned by the failure of Rolls-Royce, the non-competitiveness of Concorde. It was an expert who had been called in to axe the railways and cut their losses, it was a concatenation of experts who clamoured for their re-expansion on subsidy. They had on the whole watched without understanding or interest the reorganization of the National Health Service and of local government in ways whose only certain short-term effect was to send the staffs of both into a whirligig of job hunting and substantially to increase the salaries of most of them. More significant perhaps was the Poulson affair which revealed to all what many had feared, that not only were the power élites taking wrong decisions on behalf of the public, they were taking them on grounds of their own self-interest. Poulson's own net of corruption was extensive enough; what sent cold shivers down the public spine was his own defence that, compared to others, his operations were hardly noticeable.

Small wonder, then, that there is a muted but persistent cry for alternative ways of handling our affairs. On the level of party politics this has been taken up by all the parties with each meaning something different by it. The Liberals, having rediscovered the ancient truth that men care most for what touches them most nearly, have campaigned assiduously on local issues and won a large share of the poll, although without convincing many constituencies that they would translate their concern with local issues into competence at handling national ones. The Labour party (or at least some parts of it) talk earnestly about open government and the Conservatives passed legislation opening local council affairs to public observation. The Nationalists and Loyalists pin their faith to various forms of devolution of power from central to 'regional' assemblies.

Yet in spite of all this piety it is hard to see where changes will actually be made. In the House of Commons itself a growing executive increasingly muzzles not only its members but those who most wish to join them. Moreover, the sheer size of many of the decisions which government must make and the long time it takes to make those decisions effective reduces the capacity for individual members to affect them even if they understand them. The decision to build a Channel tunnel may be taken by one government, the tunnel will only be open (if at all) three or four governments later. If to this is added the growing interdependence of this country and others, whether through the European Economic Community or not, it is hardly surprising that back-bench M.P.s begin to seek restlessly for a new role in which to shine.

What might that role be? Surely to take a leading part in creating in his constituency the kind of information net and sense of community which will allow his constituents to understand and comment upon the important matters of the day. It may be said that this is what happens with a good member now, but if it does it is rare. The way in which most nonmarginal constituencies operate ensures that, provided a member appears occasionally, and does nothing particularly unacceptable to his local supporters, he will be adopted and returned for as long as he chooses to stand even if he speaks seldom and cuts no sort of national figure. How many M.P.s believe that it is their duty to go further than merely to listen to their constituents when the latter take the initiative in approaching them? The normal pattern seems to be one in which, except on very special issues (usually ones peculiarly dear to the heart of the M.P. or his constituents) the M.P. is felt to have discharged his duty if he appears reasonably regularly before the constituency faithful and recounts what *has been* happening. The Burke-ian tradition of the M.P. taking the decisions on behalf of his constituents, whether he has fully consulted them or not, lingers on even in days when the whips, the executive, the complexity and number of the issues have all conjoined to render it largely out of date. Yet in every constituency an M.P. could find, if he wished, 'experts' on almost every issue on which he might wish to be informed. Men and women who until now have usually felt that politics was outside their concern and that their contribution would not only never be sought but would be ignored if it were offered. It would be difficult and sometimes threatening for members of Parliament to hold regular, contentious meetings with their constituents yet nobody is better placed to foster the development of such community involvement and as experiment proceeded the boundaries within which it could be expected to be mutually profitable would certainly emerge.

If there is a need for a new kind of relationship between the M.P. and his constituents how much more so between the local government councillor and his! In far too many instances, the traditional situation has been that the newly-elected councillor, who has won his seat mainly on his devotion to the individual annoyances suffered by his constituents, turns up in the council chambers ready to battle to the death on issues of similar scale but quite unwilling or unable to take issue with the paid staff of the council on the matters of major policy. It was the Maud Committee's hope that reorganization would not only attract councillors of larger view but would free them to leave the details to the officers and thus allow them to concentrate on policy making. It remains to be seen whether their hope is justified or whether councillors of similar calibre to those of the past will find themselves gazing with even greater incomprehension than before at issues of much larger scale. Whatever happens, two things are certain. First, it will take a much more positive effort on the part of the new councillors than was necessary before if they are not to lose touch entirely with their constituency. Second, unless they take effective steps to consult their local community they will have no advice available against which to measure the opinion being assiduously fed to them by their professionals. These, however keen they may be to be objective, will have the vested interest of seeing that that the plan to which they have given most attention passes through the Council.

Moreover, each professional will be restricted, more or less, by the blinkers of his own discipline and, although machinery has been established in each local authority to diminish the dangers which arise from this, the fact remains that only one section of our society can hope to experience continuously and directly the effects of the fragmentation of the profession and of the services in which they work. This is the public itself. The public pays for the services, enjoys or suffers their attentions and in a multitude of guises helps or hinders them in the attainment of their goals. Yet the public's opinion is seldom heard, seldom sought and virtually never taken into account when the goals are being set or the machinery to achieve them being established.

At the beginning of the Welfare State it was perhaps believed that public ownership was sufficient in itself to guarantee that the public interest would at all times be safeguarded and high standards both of policy making and of execution be observed. Yet, whatever may have been the hopes at the beginning, disenchantment with public services grew rapidly until we have arrived at a point when the statutory services are often seen as undemocratic, remote, and sometimes even oppressive. Road developments, compulsory purchase orders, evictions from council housing are all features of the public sector alone and often cause as much distress or opposition as private landlords or racketeering estate agents.

In the face of all this, disenchanted with conventional politics,

constantly confronted with unwanted *faits accomplis*, the public
has responded by taking matters into its own hands, and substantially bypassing the traditional political processes. There
can be no doubting the astonishing growth of local mechanisms
for coping with local problems. Tenants' associations are daily
chalking up notable victories over harassing landlords or
obdurate councils. Claimants' unions, community schools,
amenity societies, consumer groups : the list is endless, the
activity diverse in kind, variable in effectiveness but all of it
demonstrating a new resurgence of self-reliance among the public
which conventional politicians will ignore at their peril. Along-
side this haphazard growth is an equally diverse but slightly
less ragged increase in the involvement of the voluntary or
'non-statutory' sector with the social services in our society.
The nature of voluntary activity is changing. The attraction of
the great uniformed organizations is perhaps diminishing or at
least coming down the age range. The contribution in grant aid
of the government (local and central) increases as its own
activities help to dry up the traditional sources of philanthropic
cash. The number of volunteers working in the National Health
Service, the social service departments, the probation service,
with children's panels in Scotland or with schools, immigrants,
illiterates and many others increases rapidly. Sometimes the
enthusiasm outruns the skills but every year sees more 'ordinary'
citizens playing an active part in improving the services available to the rest of us. And as they grow more sophisticated so,
of course, do the voluntary organizations through which many
of them give their services. Bodies like the Child Poverty
Action Group, Disablement Income Group, or Shelter have
served warning on the bureaucracy that slipshod statistics, un-
feeling administration or merely neglect will not necessarily go
unexposed. Even more important, many such bodies have
notable legislative changes to their credit. In their turn, voluntary
bodies are learning that horror campaigns, exaggerations and
battles fought with no understanding of the problems facing
the statutory bodies cause only harm both to their own clients
and to the voluntary sector as a whole.

People are talking increasingly of jobs which not only can
be done by volunteers but can be better done by them. Politicians
and administrators are relying upon voluntary organizations for

information, advice and political support. Moreover, both statutory and voluntary policy makers are beginning to see that much can be achieved if only the people in a particular locality can be helped to mobilize their skills, knowledge and concern in the locality itself to produce a better environment. What is needed is a focus for the manifold activities and interests within each locality. And such a focus must be able to link with its opposite numbers in other localities for many of the problems of contemporary life affect dozens of localities simultaneously. Of course, there will not always be agreement and later in the book I look at some of the difficulties caused by disagreement. Often there will be no choice or very little open to the policy makers. Sometimes a community will want responsibility for its own affairs, sometimes it will grow bored or frightened and long to give it to someone else. At present, such a development has always meant an irrevocable transfer of power from the community to the statutory authorities. Must such transfers in future be always one way and always permanent?

This book is deliberately cautious in the practical steps which it proposes. This is because I believe we have a very great deal to learn about a new form of politics and that too radical an initiative too early will prove so frightening both to those who hold power and to those who seek it that the whole policy would go into terrified reverse. But I also fervently believe that these first steps towards establishing an effective, flexible, permanent mechanism for allowing the people not only to be heard but also to be powerful in the decisions which are made on its behalf are of fundamental importance to the future of democracy in Britain. What has been given by new legislation already passed for Scotland but proposed for the rest of the country, is a chance to create a national forum for the common man. It will be fed from thousands of local forums, it will vary in strength and effectiveness as the public interest in it ebbs and flows, but if we lay the first bricks well we may build a wall which will protect democracy in Britain from the forces which have destroyed it in so many other places.

1
The Community Council

There is a new Act upon the Statute Book: the Local Government (Scotland) Act 1973,[1] and although most people will never have heard of it and few will even notice when it begins to take effect, it contains within it a provision of potentially revolutionary effect. Section 5 lays upon the new second tier local authorities (the district councils) an obligation to create a 'community council' wherever twenty or more local people demand one. In other words, all over Scotland, from Orkney to Coldstream, in country and city there will appear, under statute, new structures of government unlike anything that has ever been created in Britain before.

No statutory limits have been set upon a community council's activities; it may 'take such action in the interests of its community as appears to be expedient and practicable'. No rules are prescribed as to how it must be formed but one general purpose is defined for it: 'to ascertain, co-ordinate and express to the local authorities for its area, and to public authorities, the views of the community which it represents, in relation to matters for which those authorities are responsible'.[2] A most unusual proposition it is, and without some prior discussion and some early information about it how can the public be expected to extract the maximum benefit from it? If no attempt is made to alert people to the possibilities hidden in this seemingly minor section of an enormous and technical Act, cautious advice based on inappropriate traditions and ineffective examples from the past will be the only influences shaping the new system; potentially the best instrument for real community participation in local affairs yet created in the U.K.

It is my hope that at a time when England is struggling to find an appropriate way of bridging the abyss which gapes between the planners and the people in her cities and housing estates, and when the Welsh have already begun to form their own type of community councils, some of the speculations here, based largely but not entirely upon the Scottish scene, will have significance for other parts of Britain.

I begin by looking briefly at what is meant by participation, since if the community councils are really to assist in securing more participation it is important to know what it is that we are to have more of, even though it is tempting to agree with Hatch[3] when he writes 'discussion of participation has now continued long enough to make it more important to ask how rather than why'.

By participation I mean simply that those on whose behalf a decision is taken, or who will be directly affected by it, have some influence upon the decision makers. I have elsewhere[4] suggested a number of degrees of participation, and with some modification they may serve as a starting-point for us now. Community participation may be taken to mean:

1 Passively listening to the exposition of other people's plans which affect the community,
2 Actively helping directly in the making of such plans,
3 Helping by proxy or through representatives in the making of plans,
4 Actively helping in the execution of such plans, however made,
5 Helping indirectly in the execution of plans,
6 Commenting upon the execution of plans,
7 Exercising power to obtain changes in plans (especially for resource allocation) made by others,
8 Allocating resources,
9 Allocating and expending resources.

Let us look briefly at each of these.

1 Passively listening to the exposition of other people's plans which affect the community

This is the commonest species of the genus 'participation'. It usually means that the plan makers (who have worked away often with a minimum of consultation except with a selected group of other professionals) present an almost completed plan at a public meeting or exhibition. There is usually only one plan and both the time and place of the consultation are determined by the plan makers. Since time and place affect both who comes and what they say about the plan it is obvious that the vital initiatives all lie with the planners. In such exercises the suggestion by members of the community of more than minor alterations creates such difficulties for the planners in terms of professional and political commitment to the original plan, timing deadlines and cost increases consequent upon delay, that they are very seldom accepted.

The Skeffington Report[5] explained the consequences of such behaviour:

> Some of the authorities who have made intensive efforts to publicize their proposals have done so when those proposals were almost cut and dried. At that stage, those who have prepared the plan are deeply committed to it. There is a strong disinclination to alter proposals which have been taken so far; but from the public's point of view the opportunity to comment has come so late that it can only be an opportunity to object. The authority is then regarded more as an antagonist than as the representative of the community and what was started in good will has ended in acrimony.

Moreover, in many communities the expertise necessary fully to understand the effects of a large plan is lacking. How many ordinary members of the public know, for example, that in order to obtain any idea at all what it would feel like to walk among the buildings shown in the meticulously made scale model it is necessary to look at them on eye level? How many exhibitions mount their model lay-outs at eye level (with stairs to allow for study from above)? And yet how often will members of the public see their environment from the air? (Unless we have a touching faith in the omniscience of plan makers we can surely reject this as a model of participation.)

2   Actively helping directly in the making of plans

This was what the Skeffington Report seems to have wanted. Through community forums and other machinery the public were to be brought into the plan-making process from the earliest stage, when the plans were really fluid and commitment to any one proposal had not formed. The public was to contribute both through the numerous local societies, who were to arrange surveys, organize exhibitions and distribute publicity, and individually through public meetings. The Report was not particularly specific about the nature of an individual's contribution. Indeed, it seems to have expected that much of the public's participatory activity would consist of creating opportunities for the public to participate (and so on *ad infinitum*?). It was quite clear that 'public involvement at the formative stage in the making of a plan *in no way* [my italics] diminishes the responsibility of the elected representatives to make the final decision about the content of a plan'. In fact, it went a lot further and declared that, 'they, too, must be given the responsibility for deciding the best methods and timing of participation activities in their area'.

This was an attempt by the Committee to resolve one of the hardest of all the dilemmas which confront the advocate of participation: that consultation followed by amendments to plans followed by further consultation can continue until any opportunity for action has long melted away. Moreover, whence comes the mandate of those who would amend the plan unless, like those who have the power to *take* the decision, they have founded their claims upon some recognized authority? For Skeffington, the difficult question of whether our contemporary society is content to allow authority to reside with those who have achieved it in traditional (but no longer uncriticized ways) was inappropriate and in the short term we may, at least in part, agree with him; but, although this book is basically conservative because it is concerned with making the most of opportunities in the next few years, we cannot ignore the fact that for many people the debate over participation is more about the validity of the authority under which decision makers act, than about the nature of the decisions taken.

The Report also virtually omitted the question of the costs involved in making the wrong decision or a decision which, however correct, was made without any attempt to involve the public. What Verba (1961) calls the 'participation hypothesis', that 'significant changes in human behaviour can be brought about rapidly only if the persons who are expected to change participate in deciding what the change shall be and how it shall be made',[6] was to a large extent ignored in the Skeffington Report.

3 Helping by proxy or through representatives in the making of plans

In its simplest forms this is the democracy we have now. We elect small groups of people who make plans for us. The more time they spend making plans, the less time they have to consult us, and the more time they spend with us the less likely they are to be serious contenders for important positions in the plan-making hierarchy. The consequences of this situation are shown well by the former pattern of local government elections where 'participation' at the ballot box was seldom more than about forty-seven per cent and sixty-three per cent of members were unopposed.[7] Yet it is possible to be much less democratic even than this, where at least everyone has a chance to show his opinion of the candidates or to offer himself as one where none exists. In enterprises where the dominant groups have persuaded the government that their skills are so uniquely complex that democracy is irrelevant (the National Health Service, nationalized industries, etc.), the public's representatives on the plan-making body are not elected at all, but are appointed by the appropriate minister. Since in neither case is it normal in this country to provide the 'representatives' with any paid assistance in consulting their 'constituents', the latter can hardly be said to be secure in their participation in plan making.

An even less participatory model which comes under this heading is that of the 'consultative group' set up, usually in response to an arbitrary, if shrewd, political instinct, to enable a minister to 'take soundings'. This is a process of asking the 'people-who-matter' on the pretext that they are the same as the 'people-who-know'. Usually, such devices are used rather to sell a plan which has already been almost finalized than genuinely to seek advice or assistance. Usually, too, this process gives a second chance to the professional and other groups (such as trades unions), who have often already had an opportunity to contribute to the plan at an early stage, to press their special interest and does nothing at all to involve the public outside the circle of those already known to the planners.

4   *Actively helping in the execution of such plans, however made*

There are two ways in which this form of participation is most commonly achieved. The first is through the delegation of agency powers, with widely varying degrees of freedom of action. Thus the care of many disabled persons is largely delegated by local authorities to the voluntary bodies set up to cater for their needs and, apart from the generalized controls inherent in the giving of local authority grants, control over the agency function is usually confined to inspections and other devices concerned more with the maintenance of minimum standards than with the promotion of a comprehensive policy. In most such cases the 'community' itself is even more remote from the operation than it is from most of the plan-making operations described earlier, since those who pay for the service not only do not use it themselves, but in practice they have no say in the appointment of those who run it on their behalf.

While agency functions of this sort are coming increasingly under scrutiny as local authorities ask themselves if they could make better use of their budgets if they were to keep them in their own hands, a variant of this type of participation is becoming a little more common. The use of volunteers in the social services is markedly on the increase (see, for example, the pilot schemes for supporting Children's Hearings[8] with specially selected volunteers or the fact that volunteer bureaux now number over ninety). Occasionally the users of services themselves are beginning to be included in the execution of the policies made on their behalf, such as, for example, the patient groups who in some places organize important parts of mental hospital activity.

Indeed, it seems probable that one of the more important developments in the provision of social services in the next few years will be the growth of lay involvement. This has always been very large at the top, where policy decisions are usually in the hands of laymen; what is happening now is an increase in lay participation at lower levels. Arrangements vary from service to service and from place to place. Some hospitals make extensive use of volunteers to perform functions for which the paid staff have no time even when they have the inclination. Others come close to delegating to voluntary groups who have specialized in this kind of caring, such responsibilities as arranging for parents to visit their children. There are signs that some of the jobs which used to be performed by the statutory social service agencies may be handed back to voluntary organizations, at least in the short term, while the National Health Service and the local authorities sort themselves out after reorganization. After-care, intermediate care, welfare rights are among the services which may be given to voluntary agencies where suitable ones exist. This movement receives considerable impetus from the growing professionalism of the headquarters' staffs of many voluntary bodies. Indeed insistence upon the voluntary character of their activities frequently gives place to emphasizing their role as independent and sometimes critical partners in the provision of services. Age Concern is a good example of this.

5 *Helping indirectly in the execution of plans*

This, too, is a small but growing form of participation, and there are now numerous instances of community centres and other amenities being handed over by the local authority to residents' groups who are normally elected by the community to serve on the committee of management.

The benefits of this model are plain enough: the decisions about the day-to-day operation of the facility are taken by people near enough to the users of the facility to be recognized, and who are, theoretically, more approachable. The dangers are more philosophical but can prove real enough. As Bulpitt describes them, 'It is true that the individual may be protected from external predators (by a local operation) but internally his freedom of operation may be severely limited. In practice, the liberty protected may be not so much that of the individual as the corporate liberty of the local government.'[9] One of the strongest pressures towards centralized government was exerted by those who appealed to it against the tyranny of those nearer to them.[10] Yet at a time when statutory departments grow ever more burdened such participation might well be tried on a very much larger scale.

6   *Commenting upon the execution of plans*

One of the least successful forms of participation is that in which members of the public are placed on bodies within a service or agency whose function is primarily to comment upon its performance especially as it affects the consumer in his day-to-day dealings with the organization. Consumer councils in the nationalized industries are one example, but the National Health Service provides another (see Chapter Three) of potentially equal inadequacy. Quite apart from all their other disadvantages,[11] such bodies are even more vulnerable to lack of adequate information than most, and as Klein[12] points out with reference to the N.H.S., large parts of their obligations are rendered almost impossible to discharge because of the scarcity of information available to them. Moreover, their reports go not to the community at large but to those responsible for the service in the first place, so that the public may reasonably feel somewhat uneasy about their effectiveness.

7   *Exercising power to obtain changes in plans (especially for resource allocation) made by others*

This seems to be an increasing model for participation, and includes activities such as rent strikes, designed to compel the local authority to allocate more resources to one area in preference to another, or boycotts of schools. These activities are, of course, strictly illegal (or at least subject to legal counter-action), but in practice can be as effective as similar actions in an industrial dispute (from which they clearly derive).

Nevertheless, all these seven (and I am conscious of the artificiality of some of the distinctions which I have made) fall under the heading of what Pateman, modifying French, Israel and Aas, calls 'partial participation', i.e. 'a process in which two or more parties influence each other in the making of decisions but the final power to decide rests with one party only'.[13]

This brings us to our last two categories of participation:

8 *Allocating resources*; and 9 *Allocating and expending resources*

For many these are the only categories worth bothering about. Yet to accept this is to raise yet again all the great unanswered (and therefore unanswerable?) questions of political theory. If the community as a whole is to have power to change the allocation of resources in any but one of the traditionally indirect ways, how will it decide which parts of itself to benefit? As Klein[14] points out, participation by itself may well make for an even less defensible inequality in resource allocation than the hard to penetrate but reasonably humane bureaucracy achieves at the moment. It is not the weak and active who participate most effectively, and total participation looks very much like the margin of the pool at Bethesda[15] at which only those quick and strong enough to push aside the less agile obtained any benefit. It was, after all, Rousseau[16] himself who declared that pure democracy was workable only by gods, and there is no sound empirical evidence available to refute him. To accept this is not, however, to accept that the present system is the best possible, nor that it is as securely rooted in public esteem as it perhaps once was.[17] In numerical terms alone, the ratio of elected representatives to electors has fallen steeply in recent years in central government and the reorganization of local government imposes far more swingeing cuts in the ratios at that level.[18] Moreover, despite the hopes of the Maud Committee[19] and the Royal Commissions, it seems improbable that the time required of local councillors will diminish, particularly as the number and complexity of the decisions facing them increase. The consequence is that a smaller clique, representing much larger areas, will spend even less time than hitherto with local groups, still less with unorganized individuals, and their usefulness as communicators of local feelings or opinions will correspondingly shrink.

Yet I think that it would be unhelpful at this stage to spend too long upon the possibilities of transferring power to communities organized quite differently from the present system. To change as drastically as that would require a revolution and there is little evidence to support a proposition that in the short term at least revolutions result in large-scale power sharing. As

Dennis Kavanagh[20] argues, 'Rarely has the collapse [of regimes in new states] come because of popular pressures; rather has it come from a coup by one of the élites, normally the army.'

Consequently for the purpose of this book I shall leave on one side the question of full participation and accept that what we must consider is some degree of partial participation. In order to try to assess how large a degree we should aim for we need to answer the second of our questions: why seek participation at all?

The first answer is that to involve a much larger number of people in the formulation of the basic problems which planners need to answer, as well as in the answering of them, may well widen the perceptions of both the planners and the public of what the questions and the possibilities really are. The technicalities of planning must undoubtedly be left to trained people, and if there is to be formulated any realistic detailed alternative to highly technical plans it must be created by other specialists, whether as a kind of counter-profession outside the circle of the planning authority itself or as an expensive, but perhaps justifiable, duplicate effort within it. Both the expense and the effectiveness of such alternative efforts were well demonstrated in the hard fought campaign to persuade the government to realign the runway at Turnhouse Airport, Edinburgh. Yet to say that the technicalities of plan making usually require trained specialist or team of specialists assemble to tackle a particular described as 'the ordinary public') have nothing to contribute. Specialists have their weaknesses and laymen their strengths. A specialist is, by definition, a non-specialist in every subject but his own. Moreover, it is often as much a matter of historical accident as of contemporary appropriateness that a particular specialist, or team of specialists assemble to tackle a particular problem. For example, where a problem can be shown to have even a remotely medical component a doctor is always consulted. A nurse usually is not, and, until recently, social workers probably would not have been. This is as much a statement of the ages of the professions as of the constituents of the problem under consideration. As specialisms grow more and more narrow, it becomes harder for individual specialists to take an overall view of a problem or, indeed, even to formulate the problem in terms wide enough to match the real life situation. There is a natural tendency in all of us to define questions in ways which make it reasonable to suppose that we can seek an answer within the knowledge of ourselves and our trusted colleagues. To do otherwise is to risk a contribution from outsiders which will not only expose us as ignorant, but may result in our losing control of the answer-seeking process.

The arbitrary division of functions within local authorities, largely on the basis of traditional professional groupings, further exaggerates the haphazardness of team composition. One has only to look at the differences of approach towards community service provision among education authority community workers and social work department ones to see how much at the mercy of the original selection of plan-making personnel the public is. Moreover, to rely upon even an unusually widely qualified team is to make two assumptions, neither of which is justified by experience. The first is that the specialists assembled represent either the best or the most widely held opinions within their own specialisms. Even if they were once in the vanguard of their profession they may well have fallen behind and, as Professor Specht once put it, 'experts may suffer from hardening of the categories'.[21] The furious arguments which rage within the various professional bodies are evidence enough of the widely differing views held, and it is entirely fortuitous (at least from a particular community's point of view) which views will be in the ascendant in any particular plan-making team.[22] The second assumption is beautifully exposed in the Shelter Neighbourhood Action Project (S.N.A.P.) Report:[23] 'It is still assumed that the standards of professional élitist groups are a consensus model for all groups and, by pursuing them, social conditions will inevitably improve.' As that report showed again and again, what the public (in this case the residents of Granby) thought about their home area and what they wanted in it were often radically different for hard-headed practical reasons from what the specialists provided for them.[24]

What, then, are the strengths of the layman? They include personal involvement and personal knowledge of at least some aspects of the problems under consideration. They may also include relevant specialist knowledge or experience far outside the narrow circle of those likely to be consulted in the ordinary course of events. And, in the mass, they provide a far wider spectrum of opinions and skills than any plan-making team, however large, can hope to muster. It is for this last reason that we can share the doubts of G. D. H. Cole when he maintained that it was mistaken to assume that an individual could be represented as a whole. We may have faith in the capacity of someone to represent our views in relation to schools, but have no faith in him as our representative in relation to licensing laws or motorway designing, since none of us is wholly predictable in our responses to different situations.

The personal involvement and personal knowledge of the lay public is all-important. It may be true, as so many studies have suggested, that people's commitment to participation depends on how much chance they perceive of participating effectively—of actually changing the plan or obtaining more resources for their needs—but what is incontrovertible is that those past whose bedroom windows the new road is to go feel the problem a great deal more directly than the plan-makers. The personal knowledge of the layman is equally undeniable. Every councillor knows that the local knowledge of the residents in his or her area is formidable and vital to the success of any plan for the area. As community development projects multiply, it is also obvious that the local knowledge of those who do not naturally participate in local activities in a group or organized way is just as valuable as that of those who do. (It was a wide range of local people and not only the district *councillors* of Aviemore who suggested that the new road to the ski slopes would need larger culverts the year before it was swept away in the rain.) To tap this unorganized local knowledge positive and unconventional effort is required.

Even in the most deprived and despairing areas specialist knowledge, too valuable to ignore, is likely to abound. Much of it will be knowledge gained in conventional work, and to plan a new play facility for the area without even offering an opportunity for those who know the local children really well (such as the health visitor, primary school teachers—current or retired—the park attendant or the janitor of the secondary school) may be to miss advice which could save a serious error of design or of placing. Similarly, every area will contain people with different types of non-specialist, but valuable knowledge. Some will have lived in the locality for many years and will be able to contribute to the pool of information available to the plan makers a biased but extraordinarily deep-rooted understanding of its characteristics and points of strength and weakness. Moreover, they may be particularly well placed to define for the plan makers the problems which need to be tackled. Others may have settled there after a lifetime of travelling and will be able to comment upon a plan by comparing it with similar projects seen elsewhere. Individual councillors, officials or consultants may be able to afford to travel to three or four interesting areas to observe schemes which, with modification, might transplant into their own areas. They can spare neither the time nor the money to build up experience comparable with that of a community in which perhaps two or three hundred members have personal knowledge of situations in other parts of the country (or, indeed, in this era of world-wide air travel, of the world).

If, then, I have made out a case for the involvement of the community in the definition of problems and the making of plans, why not go further and suggest that substantial administrative responsibility be handed over to the local community? I have touched on this before and frankly admit that it poses an awkward dilemma. I believe that in areas where a sufficiently representative group is put up by the community to administer some statutory responsibilities they should be allowed to take the job on although, as we have seen, this can create serious problems, especially when the administration fails to give satisfaction to the wider community. What I am not happy about is any suggestion that the community council itself should undertake such responsibility. The chief reason for the exclusion of executive activity is the one which Lord Beveridge pointed out so clearly in *Voluntary Action*[25] long ago: if a body has co-ordinating and similarly unquantifiable functions to perform as well as executive duties it will inevitably come to concentrate upon the latter. There are many councils of social service which illustrate the truth of this. When it comes to deciding whether money should be spent to make good a lack in some local service or facility (a lack which may have been the cause of growing complaint) or on staff or equipment to make possible discussions of common problems or the formulation of comments upon some local authority plan, it is an unusually determined body of trustees or managers which chooses the latter.

I discuss in some detail later (see Chapter 2) how the community might be directly involved in the making of plans, but it is worth saying a little more here about the possible ways of enabling the community to comment upon the execution of the plans once made. We have already seen that a major advantage of community participation is that it can provide some antidote to the arbitrary divisions of administrative responsibility created by the local government committee system and, even more, by the equally arbitrary divisions between those services which are administered by the local authority and those run by central government (e.g. supplementary benefits) or *ad hoc* authorities (e.g. the National Health Service). It is only at the local, community level that the impact of the often almost independent policies of the housing, planning, health, education and income maintenance authorities are experienced and can be evaluated. It is, after all, well enough known already that the evictions policy of housing authorities has far-reaching effects upon the work of social work departments, whose own policies towards debtor clients may be equally affected by current local policies of the Department of Health and Social Security. The reorganization of social work in both England and Wales and in Scotland was designed to make easier the creation of area teams in which locally based social workers would learn their areas well enough to be able to speak from equal local experience with the doctors, teachers, health visitors and local residents. To draw upon this detailed understanding both to improve their own policy making and the quality of the information they feed up to the policy makers of the regional authority. Yet as I have pointed out elsewhere[26] one ironical result of all the reorganizations which have recently been carried out is to accelerate the already rapid turnover of professional staff. Instead of areas benefiting from the long involvement of high quality staff, the latter are being enticed—by the glowing prospects offered by headquarters teams in training, management and research—to leave the area offices even more quickly than they might have done before. As I suggested there, it will probably be necessary to look again both at the levels of salary and of responsibility for leading staff situated in area offices. When we add to this the notorious fact that staff turn-over is more rapid in deprived areas we are confirmed in our belief that a permanent and more widely representative body in each locality is essential if the plan makers are to receive the long-term, comprehensive, detailed knowledge of how their policies *as a whole* are affecting local populations. Such a body could be the community council.

If the local community, through its community council, is to monitor the execution of policies within its area, it will need a great deal of information presented to it in more digestible form than is commonly made available by local authorities and other departments at present. This means both written and graphic material of the kind described in Chapter 5 and informed discussion of the kind which best arises from multi-disciplinary meetings between lay members of the community and officers from the several departments. An organization based on the community as a whole is uniquely well placed to convene meetings which cut across all the ordinary boundaries. (This was well shown in Liverpool by S.N.A.P., where officers of the local authority were provided with unusual opportunities to work together on common problems at S.N.A.P. meetings[27] and the same phenomenon has been demonstrated at meetings con-vened by voluntary organizations in Edinburgh and elsewhere.) Such a combination of good information and the chance to question it with the officials responsible for producing it will certainly increase the power of a community council to act as the advocate for its own community. Moreover, the advantage is far from being in one direction only. Not only will the officials obtain a much clearer picture of the impact of their policies upon the local communities, but they will also acquire a much greater understanding of the link between their own depart-ment's policy and those of their colleagues. If, in addition, the community council includes in its deliberations professional workers from outside the local authority, such as the general practitioner, the value of the meetings to both 'sides' will be enhanced still further. But before we applaud the development unreservedly let us look at one difficulty.

This intensely local activity takes place at what Professor Donnison calls the 'micro-political' level and in his paper 'The Micro-Politics of the Inner City'[28] he argues that there are three things which need to be combined at it. They are

1   Better public services,
2   Accountable political leadership,
3   Effective advocacy of local views and needs.

Because the middle-class areas are likely to be more effective at participation than the deprived areas and therefore likely to obtain an even greater share of the available resources than under a non-participatory system, Professor Donnison argues that where the three aims conflict priority should be given them in the order stated. This seems to me to be a recipe for ineffective participation. Unless the middle-class areas, who often feel just as alienated from the plan makers, and just as baffled by the institutional obstacles to understanding and influencing plans as other localities, are encouraged to throw their influence behind the demand for effective participation, the new local authorities will see no reason to take it seriously. Indeed, in many areas an automatic linking of participation with a clamour for major redistribution will suffice to render it unacceptable. The question of redistribution of resources is, of course, central to all policy making, but it is something which must grow out of the general political will and in the formation of that participation in plan making is an indispensable aid. Only thus can the plan makers learn what the public wants and needs. To suggest that, because redistribution may sometimes be hampered by effective participation, the latter should be relegated to the bottom of the priority list is to despair of democracy as an effective means of allocating resources. Moreover, it is not merely in the field of public services that more participation is required or improvements needed. Many of the decisions which fundamentally affect our lives are taken by bodies over which local authorities or government departments exercise minimal control. Effective community councils would presumably concern themselves with oil companies and private developments as well as the public authorities.

This brings us to the third of my requirements: the exercise of power to effect changes in plans—the most difficult of the three. The Wheatley Report (The Royal Commission on Local Government in Scotland, Cmnd 4150) was quite clear that community councils were to be an indispensable adjunct to the new system of local government rather than a third tier within the system and the government adhered firmly to its recommendations throughout the debates on the Bill. This is just as well. If community councils had been an integral part of the local government system they would automatically have been accorded the responsibility for those functions which the other tiers did not want or did not care about. As it is, the proposed community councils should retain the most valuable asset of voluntary associations—the power to approach the bureaucracies at several levels. It will be open to them to develop formal and informal links with either officers or elected members. Care has to be taken in making use of this power since obviously its exercise can cut at the roots of confidence built up between officials and the community council. If, in the midst of a negotiation, the community council were suddenly, without notice, to go behind the official's back to the elected member or to play one off against the other, future negotiations could hardly be carried on with mutual trust. On the other hand, this dual access is a real sanction against official inertia, and community councils, like many voluntary organizations already, will need to learn how to handle it effectively. Yet the different levels of access, to officers, representatives, managers, chairmen, M.P.s or Ministers, however valuable in themselves, do not achieve power. How can a community council make changes in plans or see that its information and views are turned into action?

The answer must lie in politics. In the end, community councils will succeed to the extent that they manage to make the political system, with all its imperfections, work for them. The councils themselves will be non-political in the sense that from most of them at least party politics will presumably be excluded. They will, however, have to command political muscle. In this, as in so much else in our subject, different levels of operation can be discerned. If the community council is successful in engaging the interest of the press and of the media, the affairs of even quite a small locality may be blazoned in ways which no politician could ignore with impunity. Yet by itself this is nothing like enough. As the S.N.A.P. Report succinctly put it, 'interests of the city as a whole were rarely, if ever, those of the people in its most deprived wards', so that if one particular community were to seek significant modifications in a

plan already made they would have to fight a political battle
over a much wider area than their purely local one. How might
this be done? First, through alliances of community councils
themselves. Where a number of community councils within a
region recognized that they had a similar problem, joint con-
sultations and activity could be arranged. (One feature of plans
which is too often forgotten is that areas which are not directly
concerned in a particular plan may nevertheless be keen to
participate in and learn from discussions of it since they expect
to be meeting similar problems shortly. Also, of course, a plan
to alter traffic flows or to change the distribution of services
may create unforeseen but semi-predictable difficulties for areas
outside the scope of the plan itself.) In Northern Ireland it was
suggested at one point that 'where at least twenty-five per cent
of the wards in a district have a similar problem and agree on
a common approach representatives of such a forum would ...
have the *right* [my italics] of consultation with representatives
of any statutory organization whose functions have a bearing on
the problem or situation'.[29] The Government has remained firm
in its refusal to grant statutory rights of consultation to community councils (see Chapter 3) in Scotland, but the effect
of a significant number of community councils banding together
would probably be the same. A regional or district grouping
of community councils with pronounced views and competent
membership could hardly be safely ignored by the regional or
district councillors.

The community councils would, similarly, be able to convene
meetings to which politicians of all parties could be invited,
chosen not, as in usual, at their initiative, but at that of the
community councils. In places where they were effective, unusual
juxtapositions of politicians dependent more on specialist expertise than on party position or label might be achieved. This
would lead to a blurring of party lines when local problems were
under discussion. It is wishful thinking to hope that parties
will grow less significant under local government reorganization,
but unless some return is made to reasonably fluid groupings
of politicians formed and reformed round common area interests
in preference to party doctrine, it is hard to see how the growing
interest in local questions will find its political outlet except in
demonstrations and disruption rather than through the electoral

process. It is, however, for the political system to adapt to this pressure rather than for it to seek to avoid it by refusing to assist community participation. Nevertheless, it is only realistic to suggest that the acquisition of power in this sense by community councils will follow the other two stages only after an interval.

We look later at the role of the councillor in all this, but we might note here that the community councils may decide to provide their local councillors with the kind of fact-finding and public relations support without which their councillor will always be weaker than the officials with whom he or she has to deal. It would obviously be up to the individual councillor to decide what use he or she might make of such assistance, but the mutual value to be derived from some such semi-structural innovation is theoretically too great to be lightly ignored.

Notes

1. Local Government (Scotland) Act. Section 51 (2).
2. Local Government (Scotland) Act. Section 51 (2).
3. S. Hatch, ed., *Towards Participation in Local Services* (Fabian Tract 419), p.4.
4. *Community Councils.* Scottish Council of Social Service, Occasional Paper No. 1, January 1973.
5. *People and Planning.* Report of the Committee on Public Participation in Planning (Ministry of Housing and Local Government, Scottish Development Council and Welsh Office) 1969.
6. S. Verba, *Small Groups and Political Behaviour.* Princeton University Press 1961.
7. See Royal Commission on Local Government in Scotland 1966-9, Cmnd 4150, paragraph 88. Since some polls were high, the average Conceals a large number of contests in which the turnout was substantially lower than forty-seven per cent.
8. The Children's Hearings are the novel system for dealing with children who are deemed to be in need of compulsory measures of care, introduced by the Social Work (Scotland) Act 1968. The system itself depends on volunteers being prepared to serve on the hearings.
9. J. G. Bulpitt, 'Participation in Local Government: Territorial Democracy' in G. Parry, ed., *Participation in Politics* (Manchester University Press 1972), p.288.
10. A good example was provided in an interview on television with a retired Chinese rickshaw puller who explained that in his block of flats tenants who neglected their flats were told their faults and given a chance to reform by a tribunal of their fellow tenants. He

did not say what happened in the event of recalcitrance but the dangers are evident enough.

11. See the Select Committee on Nationalized Industries, Cmnd 5067.

12. R. Klein, 'Health Services: The case for a counter bureaucracy' in S. Hatch, ed., *Towards Participation in Local Services*. Fabian Tract 419.

13. C. Pateman, *Participation and Democratic Theory* (C.U.P. 1970), p.70.

14. S. Hatch, ed., *Towards Participation in Local Services*. Fabian Tract 419.

15. The Gospel According to St John 5.2-8.

16. J. J. Rousseau, ed., *The Social Contract* (O.U.P. 1971), p.233.

17. In fact, it is questionable whether it ever attracted much esteem since between the introduction of adult franchise and the voicing of widespread anxieties about the democratic system there seems to be no gap.

18. Prior to the reorganization there were 5,450 elected councillors representing an electorate of 3,688,316. After the reorganization 1,623 represented the same electorate. A similar situation occurred in England outside Greater London where the number of representatives fell from 32,000 elected representatives plus 4,000 aldermen to 19,700 elected representatives.

19. Report of the Committee on the Management of Local Government. H.M.S.O. 1967.

20. D. Kavanagh, 'Political Behaviour and Participation' in G. Parry, ed., *Participation in Politics* (Manchester University Press 1972), p.110.

21. Specht, From a talk given at the National Institute of Social Work Training, 1973.

22. I have tried throughout to avoid the term 'planner' unless I mean people involved in the sort of plan making covered by the planning legislation.

23. Shelter Neighbourhood Action Project Report, 'Another Chance for Cities'. (S.N.A.P. 1972), p.27.

24. See, for example, the reaction to the proposal to provide off-street car parking which was sharply resisted because no one in Granby felt secure while their car was out of sight of their house.

25. Lord Beveridge, *Voluntary Action*. Allen and Unwin 1949.

26. A. Rowe, 'Some Implications of the Career Structure for Social Workers' in W. D. Reekie and Norman C. Hunt, eds, *Management in Social and Safety Services*. Tavistock Press 1974.

27. See report, 'Another Chance for Cities' (S.N.A.P. 1972).

28. D. Donnison, 'The Micro-Politics of the Inner City'. Paper given to B.A.A.S.A. 1971.

29. A consultative paper prepared by Professor Hywel Griffith *et al.* Spring 1971.

2
Functions and Areas

The tasks which a community council might perform will vary from time to time and place to place. They seem likely to include

1 Commenting upon plans submitted to it by other bodies,
2 Putting forward proposals to cope with problems felt by the community to be important,
3 Acting as a link between the public at large and the elected representatives and other so-called spokesmen for the community (such as representatives on local health councils),
4 Collecting and disseminating information likely to be of interest or concern to the community.

If we take these in turn, some of the criteria for establishing a community council are likely to emerge.

1 Commenting upon plans submitted to it by other bodies

We have already seen that comment on plans must, to be effective, be made at as early a stage in a plan's life as possible. It is, therefore, essential that a community council receives early warning of any plan upon which its comments are likely to be invited. It is, of course, ridiculous to suppose that every tentative plan made by the local authorities and other bodies would be submitted to the community council, or that any community council could possibly respond to continual requests for comment upon all plans no matter how trivial. Some selection must, therefore, be made; the vital question is who makes it? If the whole initiative lies always with the policy making bodies it will be very hard to ensure that the community council receives information about any plan early enough to be useful. Yet it is indisputable that a large part of the initiative is bound to remain with those who are busy formulating the plans. Some sort of compromise will have to be reached, and experience suggests that in most areas it will take a long time to achieve any substantial shift from the policy makers to the community councils. But the present belief that until a plan has been thought out in all its details it must be treated as confidential must be replaced with the idea that the more fluid a plan is the less confidential it should be. This is a hard doctrine for at least two reasons. The first is that it tends to diminish the pride of authorship. A bright bureaucrat will naturally want as many of his colleagues as possible to admire the scintillations of his intellect, and one way to achieve this is to consult them about an idea as widely as possible before clouding the pure stream of his inventiveness with the nameless contributions of unidentifiable tributaries outside the office. A second reason is the ancient problem of causing unnecessary public anxiety. There is plenty of evidence about the problems of 'planning blight'—lower prices for property caused by uncertainty about the intentions of the planning authority, etc.—but the lessons to be derived from this evidence are far from obvious. It seems at least arguable that the uncertainty which would result from early public discussion of policy alternatives would be no more damaging than the apprehensions presently caused by the secrecy which so often surrounds the formulation of local authority plans. I can see advantages in a system where it was not only the property developers who knew what was being thought about in the corridors of power. When there are several possible routes for a motorway under discussion house prices in the areas known to be threatened often drop sharply. When the decision is made, the prices in the unaffected areas recover. But if the areas were widely known people who had to sell their houses during the period when prices were depressed would suffer hardship. This is the main argument against my proposal but I suspect that a combination of rumour and secrets leaked by the unscrupulous or the indiscreet often achieve the same effect now, and under my proposal there might be some prospect of devising adequate compensation procedures since the periods of depressed price would be easily stated and unarguable. Public knowledge is often easier to handle than rumour.

2   Putting forward proposals to cope with problems felt by the community to be important

It has been well said of university teaching that 'the average curriculum consists of the answers to questions which the students have never even thought of asking'.[1] The same danger can easily arise in community participation. If community councils were to confine themselves to commenting upon plans put forward by others it is probable that public interest would usually be very low. If, however, they busied themselves with discovering and collecting information about issues which were bothering members of the community and put forward tentative ideas as to how they might be tackled, the position might change rapidly. There is plenty of evidence to suggest that local communities will display a good deal of energy if they feel that they are contributing to the solution of a problem which they themselves have discovered. For example, when in one small burgh of Scotland a working party of local people enlisted the help of the local schoolchildren to carry out a survey of accessibility for the disabled to local public buildings, the project rapidly spilled over into a survey of pedestrian crossings, high kerbs, traffic hazards for pedestrians, etc., and the final report was not only welcomed by the local authority but also substantially acted upon.[2] The good effect on the morale of all those concerned with the project was enormous and there was a good deal of pressure to find another topic on which similar action might be undertaken.

This kind of activity is particularly valuable in that it helps to overcome one of the major problems facing policy makers: the very wide gap which often exists between the expectations of the community and those of the planners. In fact, of course, it is a gap created by different levels of expertise. The planners know so much more than the public about what is technically possible and about what is likely to happen in ten years' time. But in part it is a cultural gap. A professional, middle-class planner (who may well have arrived only recently in his area) is likely to find it very difficult fully to understand the attitudes and aspirations of a mining or agricultural community even if he makes an effort to do so, and few local authority planners have the time even to try.

3 *Acting as a link between the public at large and the elected representatives, etc.*

The possibilities open to community councils in their relationship with local elected representatives and other spokesmen of the community are similar to the varieties of community participation discussed in Chapter 1 and no doubt a wide variety will be seen in practice. All I shall do here is to suggest one way in which the relationship might develop to mutual advantage. It seems to me that it will be necessary for community councils to use their representatives for their own purposes and for the representatives in turn to use the community councils similarly. The community councils will need information both about what the various authorities are doing or planning to do and about how they operate. They will want to learn whom to approach on what issues and when are the appropriate stages for the public to intervene in the policy making process; they will also want to know what effect their own activities are having and how they might achieve even better results. For his part, the representative will want information not only about community attitudes but also facts about the community. It is inconceivable that local authorities, area health boards, or central government departments will have the resources ever to discover all that they might about local communities. It would probably be highly undesirable if they could. There is a great deal which the local community either knows or could discover about itself which would be enormously valuable to a representative. In Dunblane, Perthshire, for example, the Dunblane Society (a local community group) carried out a door-to-door survey to discover the present and future educational needs of the town. Residents were much readier to provide information to local people about their likely family size than they would have been in reply to a formal questionnaire administered by a stranger. The result was much better information than could have been discovered by the education authority unaided, even supposing that it had had the resources to carry out a comprehensive rather than a sample survey. The consequence of that was a revision of the educational plan for the area which would have been beyond the capacity of the local councillor to secure without the help of the Society. In the new local authorities the councillors may conceivably have something approaching adequate secretarial assistance (it will be disgraceful if they do not), but regional or county councillors not only have enormous and often very varied areas to represent, they also have a great deal of difficult policy making to do. The need, therefore, for accurate, up-to-date information will become even greater, and the councillor who can persuade his local community councils to help him obtain it will be greatly strengthened in his policy making endeavours.

It will not be an easy outcome to achieve. For many representatives, the knowledge of how the machine works seems to be the source of power, and to share that knowledge with the community at large will seem at first to be a dangerous divestment of authority. Many councillors are going to find it hard enough to accept that many of the functions which they perform at present should be handed over to the officers. If, at the same time, they are expected to make it easier for the community to find its way around the regional and district offices they may well feel that they are inviting the public to bypass them altogether. It is a natural but ill-founded fear. It is only if the public understand much better than they do at present both the possibilities and the constraints of the system that they will be able to help their councillors by bringing to them problems appropriate to their position and information of a kind likely to assist them. These are difficult skills for both sides to learn. Early meetings between elected representatives and community councils are likely to be characterized by mutual hostility, with the community expecting too much of their councillors and the councillors responding defensively. In such circumstances it is too easy for both sides to feel that the meetings are unhelpful; for the public to be confirmed in its belief that local government is irrelevant and uncaring and for the councillors to feel that meetings of this sort are threatening and unpleasant and therefore better not held at all. Only by perseverance can mutual understanding be expected to grow, and unless it does community councils will suffer dreadfully from lack of regular contact with councillors and others. Where the relationship develops well, the councillor may often find himself protected against unjust attacks by outsiders since once it is understood where the limits of his power lie, the community will often rally to his support under attack.

4 *Collecting and disseminating information likely to be of interest or concern to the community*

In all the discussions of community councils proper emphasis has been put upon their potential information-giving function. It is no coincidence that almost the first activity in the Home Office Community Development Project areas was the publication and circulation of a newsletter, for there is no doubt that unless people know what is happening they remain prey to rumours which not only cause distress in many cases but also tend to prevent the emergence of effective community action. The question is : how should the information be collected, sifted and disseminated?

Many people believe that a part-time volunteer in each community should be found to edit a newsletter, which would consist largely of information sent in by local voluntary organizations and other groups, but which might be augmented with items contributed by the local authorities and any other bodies interested in informing the local community. Because the areas covered will be small and money short, the newsletter will be cheaply run off and distributed locally as well as may be. Such suggestions ignore the major considerations altogether.

First, there is the problem of area. If a community council newsletter is confined to a very small area news coverage is likely to be capricious. Many of the issues most likely to interest the community—schools, hospitals, etc.—will spread across several communities. Either some of the communities will receive information about the issues and others will not or they all will. If they all do, is it not sensible for them all to receive the same information? If so, this suggests a central source of information at a level higher than that of a community council area. Yet if this is accepted, is there not a danger that the entirely local concerns—the closing of a local street for repairs or recreation, the changing of the branch library opening hours—will tend to be omitted?

Second comes the problem of distribution. If a newsletter is produced, how is it to arrive in every house? Most organizations faced with such a problem operate through a system of street wardens or some similar device of making individuals responsible for a number of houses. If it were only a question of distribution, it would not matter very much what method were chosen. But, of course, there are strong arguments for linking the system with any constitutional arrangements governing the community council itself. In areas where the community council contained a representative from every street it would seem sensible to give him the duty of delivering the newsletter.

Any such arrangement would be expensive, so that the arguments for keeping the production costs to a minimum are very strong. On the other hand, why should the devil have all the best tunes? When a local authority wants to publicize itself it usually employs attractively produced literature, and there is something slightly incongruous in the servants living better than their masters.

Perhaps a solution to these problems might be sought along the following lines. Each region would establish an editorial office for a regional newsletter. This would be attractively produced at regular intervals and would contain a mass of information from both the regional and district councils, the area health boards, the local offices of the national departments, etc. It might be that each district in the region would have a separate edition. Into this publication community councils would be encouraged to insert their own contributions rather as do parishes in diocesan church magazines at present. This device would allow for coverage of the wider issues, economical but attractive printing and wide circulation of regional and district news. The question of how and by whom editors should be chosen and appointed is obviously so closely linked with other questions about a possible regional structure for community councils that it can be left till later.

If, then, these are some of the tasks which a community council might be expected to perform, what form of organization would be best fitted to discharge them?

First, the organization must be *permanent*. If it is to be effective the bodies which would seek its advice must know where and how to find it. Second, it must command the confidence of the community it serves. It would be ineffective if it appeared to be speaking only with the voice of a clique within the community. Third, it seems inevitable that it should be clearly linked with a particular area. If it is to enjoy the kind of mutual confidence with representatives elected from a particular area which has been discussed above, it seems bound to be identified with that area or a part of it.

First, permanence: the Scottish Act lays down that a community council need not exist anywhere unless demanded by the community, but lays a duty upon district councils to submit a scheme to the Secretary of State making provision for community councils throughout the district. This seems to achieve the right balance. It provides a clearcut procedure for creating community councils without forcing them upon any community, an action which would be a clear recipe for apathy. Nothing can compel a community council to be active, but unless they retain at least a residual address for receiving communications from the statutory authorities it will be hard for them to be useful, except in conditions of exceptional crisis when it is comparatively easy to summon into existence some form of community group. The need for a permanent address suggests that perhaps some unit rather larger than is often suggested as appropriate for a community council might be helpful.

Second, trust. How can the community council ensure that the community accepts what it says as the authentic voice of the community? Most people answer this question in strictly traditional terms. They see the constitution as providing the only guarantee of credibility and, as Harrison[3] has pointed out, enormous care and energy is expended on drawing up a constitution to ensure that everyone in the community has a right to elect members of the council or, in those areas where the whole community is the council, the executive committee. There are some areas (Angell in Lambeth, for example) where a deliberate attempt is made to avoid this kind of traditional élitism and all the official duties are scrupulously carried out among a changing kaleidoscope of members and everyone is entitled to vote at meetings. Yet both these solutions concentrate, at one end or the other, upon a conventional voting system, and therefore fall into two traditional traps. The first is simply one of numbers. If the community as a whole does not attend, the meetings can be regarded simply as a statement of the majority of the local zealots. The second follows from the first. If at the meetings one group of particularly persuasive residents obtains the majority of votes, those who fall frequently into the minority will cease to attend and the depleted attendance falls further with a consequent loss of credibility for the council as a mouthpiece for the area. What is required is an organization which recognizes the fact that only a very few citizens are fascinated by politics and that most would infinitely prefer to spend a hot summer afternoon making use of the local recreational facilities than sitting in a room debating whether there are enough of them. This is what the political enthusiasts call apathy and everyone else calls commonsense. Moreover, it is essential that the organization should make it possible for different views not only to be expressed but to be forwarded to the outside bodies with whom the community council is concerned. Most representative and co-ordinating bodies are too concerned to obtain consensus, in their search for which they emasculate the more vigorous opinions among their members. They would rather forward a eunuch's whisper of protest than give expression to the virile if divergent anxieties of their community. The result is that either they are ineffective or that their statements represent only a minority of their potential membership. If the statements of the community councils are forwarded as the view of the whole community but are only the views of a tiny number of members, those who know nothing about the issues under discussion, or who hold different views, are probably better to withdraw from the council and either establish some independent organization of their own or join the 'apathetic'. Obviously, if we were talking about responsibility for action the case would be different. In our present society we are not good at devising an alternative to the present system of elected representatives who can be held accountable for the policies which it is their responsibility to execute. (Unless it is felt that the alternative adopted in the National Health Service and too freely elsewhere—of giving responsibility to *ad hoc* élites leaping fully armed from the heads of Cabinet Ministers—is an improvement.) An important advantage of community or neighbourhood councils is that they do not have responsibility for the execution of policies so that voting can be an exceptional device confined to internal matters of administration. If we progress to a situation in which *power* is shared with the community at large we shall have to find ways of making the community *account-able* for the exercise of that power and more elaborate procedural rules become unavoidable. This stage, however, seems a long way off and it would be a mistake to discuss the appropriate machinery for a consultative body as if it were an executive one.

Let us look, therefore, at a possible model for the operation of community councils within a district and try to distinguish those features which might conform to general rules and those which must properly be left to local variation. Under the Act, district councils have to prepare schemes detailing the proposed areas, the representational arrangements and the financing of the community councils which might be established within their district.

Areas

The whole reorganization of local government is based upon new definitions of area and since the main channel of communication between the regional and district councils and the community is likely to remain the councillor (who is elected from a geographically defined constituency), it seems inevitable that community councils should be established on a similarly geographically determined base.

Yet however inevitable our acceptance of this we must be careful of it, for unless we are we could find that in settling for a geographical basis for the new councils we were cutting at the very roots of all that they could otherwise become. Nobody knows what a community is in a twentieth-century, post-industrial country. All geographical definitions fail, except perhaps on a scale far too large to be helpful to us. The Wheatley Commission, like its English counterpart, produced some reasonable criteria for determining the boundaries of the new upper tier authorities, but when it came to examine what community meant at the lowest level it was less certain of its ground. In Appendix Thirteen it looked at three areas of Scotland according to five groups of criteria but these resulted in sub-divisions of the areas so close to the existing ones of parish or district that their value as bases for a new structure is limited. A population range from 600 to 50,000 suggests that our ideas of what constitutes a community are unrefined.

The Maud Commission's research suggested that people's perception of a 'home area', at least in towns, ceased after they moved away more than two or three streets. Community development experience proclaims that there is hardly an area too small to contain elements of diversity so pronounced that part of the claims of any one section to be 'the community' can be overthrown as soon as anything occurs to mobilize any other.

The problem is that each of us belongs to innumerable 'communities' simultaneously and most of us, indeed, are entirely inconsistent about which 'community' matters most to us at any given moment. Even in a small, clearly defined country village the geographical boundaries will often prove misleading if they suggest a homogeneity of community spirit. Income, occupation, travelling habits, age, religion, size and composition of family are as powerful and as confusing determinants of 'community' as property location. Those who were most vocal and determined in pressing for the community centre primarily as an entertainment base for teenagers may be the first to seek to limit its use when their own teenagers have moved out of the village and the discotheques and pop-groups of their successors seem to have become the jungle noises of an alien generation. The widening of the main road through the village may seem long overdue to those who commute through it every day or who live several streets away from it, but it may be little short of a nightmare to those whose houses border it or whose shops depend not on passing but on stopping trade. These are, of course, familiar problems and the difficulty of coping with them too often leads the decision makers in society into a despairing refusal to consult the public on any but issues so tiny that either a consensus of community opinion can reasonably be expected, or a failure to achieve one is politically and practically unimportant. There are plenty of signs that the same could happen to community councils. The Convention of Royal Burghs in their evidence to the Royal Commission spoke for many[4] when they denied the need for community councils at all and sought more district councillors instead. A rigid adherence to traditional elections, based either on areas too small to be significant or too large to stand any chance of developing any real sense of community, could easily confirm the traditionalists in their presumption that community councils are doomed to fail and lead to giving them delegated powers of the most trival sort, which would occupy them totally and keep them satisfactorily out of the way of the policy makers.[5]

What creates community feeling in our mobile society are issues not areas. Those who are interested in the local hospital may be drawn from all over its catchment area and differ from each other in class, education and type of residence. But if they have been patients or visitors in the hospital or workers in the health service they will, on any issue relating to that hospital, have a common bond which could be turned into a valuable instrument of democratic participation. On that one issue they would have formed 'a community'. Even if groups of them differ over some particular issue the debate, informed by this common interest, is likely to have been valuable. The same applies to the local school, or to the bus services, to the by-pass or the bowling green. If we want to obtain the advice and to learn from the experience of the public we must recognize that different members of the public will concern themselves about different things. If, for reasons of tradition and convenience, we try to create a system wherein we turn always to the same members of the public for advice, we shall achieve neither community participation nor good advice. Those who claim to be interested in every issue tend to be principally interested in politics for their own sake and the number of issues on which they can claim to be genuinely knowledgeable in detail is as small for them as for most members of the community.

Herein lies one of our central dilemmas. How can we find a model for community councils which will allow us to accept the geographical pattern dictated to us by the rest of local government (and indeed central government) organization and which will, at the same time, enable us to collect the views of 'communities' based on very different foundations? There will need to be a good deal of local experimentation before clear answers can be supplied, but the following theoretical model contains many of the features which seem to me important.

First, size. Community council areas should normally be small, so that everyone in the area stands a reasonable chance of being able to attend meetings without much difficulty or expense. If areas are very small, two other advantages accrue :

first that most business could be handled, if desired, in plenary sessions so that the emergence of an élite is postponed, if not indeed prevented; second, most of the members of the community could have at least some knowledge of most of the others and the possibilities of important sections of opinion being passed over unnoticed will be correspondingly reduced.[6] In country areas, many of the community council areas seem reasonably established by traditional boundaries, although in some places there seem to be tentative moves by the future district authorities to group together traditional communities on grounds which seem inadequately thought out.[7] In the towns the problems are much greater. Some places, proud of their long history as burghs, are already manoeuvring (or rather, those people who currently hold positions of authority in the burghs are doing so) to ensure that the whole burgh is counted as one community council area. It will be interesting to see whether, if this policy succeeds, the public as a whole remain as apathetic as they did under the old local government system or whether the new concept arouses new interest. In the larger towns, which are obviously too big for the idea of one community council to be entertained for a moment, the problems are different again. It is tempting to accept some of the present administrative or social divisions as bases on which to found a system of community councils, but in practice these, as we already know, tend to conceal differences deep enough and clear enough to anyone intimately concerned with the area to make the idea of one council for the whole unworkable. Considerable differences in cohesion and self-confidence can exist among groups living in an outwardly homogeneous administrative unit. It is, for example, tempting to lump one large housing estate together as a single community, even though there are groups within them which feel that they by themselves make a genuine community which is, in many important respects, at odds with the rest of the estate.[8] Once again the danger is that it is too easy to assume that a community of interest on one issue (like Corporation rents policy) affecting every section of the estate, means that a genuine community for all issues can be defined by the convenient geographical boundaries.

Thus the problem in the urban areas, particularly, remains a very difficult one. Make the community council areas small enough to match most urban dwellers' perception of a home area and there is created a plethora of tiny councils, constrained to operate on voluntary labour alone, since they will not be able to command enough financial support to pay for either staff or materials. Make the areas large enough to restrict the number of community councils to manageable proportions and there is virtually no hope of their being recognized by their inhabitants as community areas. (By 'manageable proportions' I mean a number which could, physically, be attended by officers and members of the district and regional councils during the year.)

Each district will have to make its own decisions, but it is much to be hoped that schemes will propose small areas even though this will mean that the community councils will have to share many of their resources with several neighbouring councils. With all its difficulties, such a scheme offers more hope of genuine community involvement than a tidy administrative design for much larger areas.

If, then, we accept that community council areas should be kept small unless there are overriding traditional grounds for larger ones, what will happen when a considerable issue arises? If the regional council were to seek the views of the community upon the future of the city centre, or the area health board to look for help on its policy towards the outlying smaller hospitals in its area, how should they set about seeking it? It is wholly unrealistic to expect them to notify tens or possibly hundreds of community councils and equally absurd to expect that the fragmented views so gathered would be particularly useful. On such questions most very small community councils would have little experience or interest to offer on their own. Clearly some joining together of all the relevant community councils would be required; the question is: how best to secure it? This leads us straight into a discussion of the

Machinery of Community Councils

On the smallest scale, a community council might be able to manage with no more than a part-time volunteer to act as secretary. The secretary's duties would include calling the meetings, taking minutes and providing the necessary continuity between one meeting and the next. No doubt many areas would be able to find energetic and sophisticated secretaries who would be capable of undertaking a very wide range of functions and able to organize other volunteers into shouldering specialist burdens, like the production of a regular news sheet or the contribution of items to the local radio station. It would be unrealistic to expect every area to be so fortunate and many secretaries will operate at a pretty straightforward level. It would also be unreal to expect all but a tiny number of part-timers to identify, unaided, issues which went much wider than the confines of their own community and to take appropriate action on them. It will, therefore, be necessary to ensure that there is a higher level of organization. This might simply be a district office serving all the community councils in the district, or even a regional office for all the councils in the region. Perhaps ideally such a central office would grow from gradual co-operation between the small community councils, rather as the regional groupings of children's panels[9] have grown in Scotland, but it may be that more positive assistance for the new structure will be needed from the beginning.

In essence the function of the central office, whether at regional or district level, would be much the same as those postulated at the start of this chapter for community councils themselves. The office would provide a focal point through which outside bodies would approach those community councils which should be consulted on a particular issue. It would also make it easier for regional and district councillors to keep in touch with those issues and communities which were of particular importance at any given moment. Above all, the central office would be able to act as a centre for the collection and dissemination of information. If the idea of a regional or district newsletter with local inserts were accepted, it would be edited here. It would also be part of the central office's task to monitor the proceedings of its regional and district councils, through the minutes and in other ways, in order to be able to alert local councils about issues which might affect them at once or in the future. Rather as the central office of the Citizens' Advice Bureaux issues its Citizen's Advice News Service (C.A.N.S.) with their invaluable mixture of information and advice, so the regional community council office would issue regular statements about changes in the law (whether national or local). So, too, it would be in a position to assist in the convening of joint meetings of a number of community councils affected by a common issue. A proposal to change the local bus schedule or make comprehensive some local schools could be discussed at a large joint meeting organized by the central office. Thereafter, the meeting itself would take over appointing appropriate working groups or delegating tasks to appropriate members. This would satisfy both the necessity for local community councils to run their own affairs and the need to release the central office staff for other functions which can only be performed at the centre.

The proposal to establish regional (or at least district) offices raises two major issues. The first: whether the successful creation of a small number of effective focuses for community participation on a scale hitherto hardly imagined and certainly unpractised would lead logically and appropriately to the establishment of a national centre. If it did, what relation would such a centre bear to a Scottish Assembly and other national institutions? These questions must be dealt with in a separate chapter. The second issue concerns the control of the regional centre, raising in starker form the issue of the control of the local community councils which it would exist to serve.

I have already suggested that traditional elections would merely create an illusion of participation in most areas. The establishment of a small élite, no matter how representative it at first appeared, would lead speedily to the kind of inadequate opinion gathering and hence impotence which is one of the main reasons for the failure of the present local government system to involve the public. Yet satisfactory alternatives are hard to find. 'Representation' through the election or co-option of members of local groups suffers from two disadvantages. It does nothing to avoid the creation of an élite, even though it goes some way to ensure that the élite is broadly based. More seriously, it does nothing to make it easy for the non-joiners, the large number of people who are not interested in joining, still less in running organizations, to play their full part.[10] Yet their experience on a particular issue might be enormously valuable.

There really seems to be no satisfactory alternative to a Rousseau-ish gathering—a public meeting open to everyone in the area. In most cases this would mean everyone whose normal home lay within the area, but it would be up to each community to make its own rules. In commuter areas it might be thought desirable to include people who lived outside the area but worked within it or to encourage the interest of those who, wherever they live, have particular connections with the community (such as parents of children in the school or users of some major community facility). Although this would mean that some people would belong to two councils and might therefore seem to be encouraging the kind of plural voting which was eradicated from the parliamentary system in 1948, the position is made wholly different, of course, by the fact that community councils are concerned with opinion and not with the exercise of power, at least directly.

The point has often been made[11] that eligibility for membership of community councils can safely ignore many of the usual rules. It would, for example, seem reasonable to admit children, since there is no substitute for the direct expression of opinion by the recipients of policies made on their behalf and many of the issues likely to interest community councils will be of direct concern to children or at least to teenagers.

So far, then, the model envisages community councils covering small geographical areas, to whose meetings all residents and certain other categories of person would be entitled to come, serviced by either a part-time voluntary secretary or a paid one who would be expected to keep in close touch with the regional office of a community councils association. This would provide advance notice of issues likely to interest the local council, information and assistance on a wide variety of matters, as requested by the constituent, councils or by outside bodies anxious to make use of the community council network to ascertain public opinion or to tap community wisdom. This structure puts a good deal of power into the hands of the secretary. Harrison[12] has shown how some London neighbourhood councils have tried various ways of ensuring that such power is not abused by becoming too remote from the community from which it derives and, as always, there are difficulties about obtaining a workable balance between continuity and efficiency on the one hand and obvious democracy upon the other. At regional level the conflict is even more obvious and important, but the problem is the same. How can the officials of the community council be controlled without their controllers becoming an élite removed, by their constant and close preoccupation with the affairs of the council, from the community? There can be no wholly satisfactory answer, but if the committee or small group to which the officials at either regional or local level are answerable are given very limited functions only, the dangers of élitism will be minimized. Their functions might be restricted to the following:

1 To raise, hold and account for any moneys on the community council,
2 To manage any properties owned by the community council and to employ any paid or voluntary staff of the council,
3 To receive and transmit (through channels agreed by the community) communications from the local authorities and other bodies,
4 To convene, or to arrange for the convening of any meeting requested by (an agreed proportion of the community),
5 To pass on to the appropriate bodies any communications as requested by the community at properly constituted meetings.

It will be seen at once that the connection between this small group and the community at large is close and continuous. On almost every matter power lies in the community meeting and not with the smaller groups and although it seems likely that in many areas the community will come to delegate more real power to the small group, at least that should be the result of increasing trust and not the consequence of an élite giving itself important powers. It may be objected that membership of such a committee promises too little reward to attract members. This is a powerful objection, but if the powers are to be so limited, the need for a large committee to ensure wide representation disappears and it should not be too hard for most communities to find three or four people prepared to serve in this important if unglamorous way.

Yet even if these safeguards are enough to secure the community council from virtually permanent domination by its trustees, the problem remains that the secretary will have considerable power. There will, after all, be very large numbers of documents such as minutes of local authority meetings, circulars, planning applications and much else passing through the secretary's hands. Often, no doubt, members of the public will demand that action be taken on one or other topic, but it is only realistic to recognize that more often the secretary will make the effective choice between taking some sort of action and doing nothing. This is the classic dilemma of participatory democracy. If nobody is ever to be in a position of superior opportunity there will be few areas in which apathy will not reign. If, on the other hand, the secretary is appointed with virtually permanent security of tenure there will be many areas in which he or she will effectively dominate the community council. The dilemma is inescapable. All we can do is to suggest two far from ideal methods of diminishing the perils.

First, it would be possible to arrange for the secretary to be elected by everyone within the community council area. Tenure would be for a limited period, perhaps as little as one year in the first place. This would certainly enable the community to rid itself of an unsatisfactory secretary. It might also ensure that very few people would bother to seek such an insecure position. After all, unlike a councillor or an M.P., the secretary would have virtually no policy making powers so that the job would not even have that attraction.

A second possibility was raised in the early discussions of the original circular on community councils.[13] This was that the secretaries of community councils should normally be drawn from a central corps of suitable people who would thus be able to look for a career in such posts. Like Procurators-Fiscal[14] they would be able to progress from small community council areas either to larger ones (if any exist) or to posts nearer the centre of a national system. Some (notably Mr Ronald Duff, then an Edinburgh City Councillor) believed that, like the procurators-fiscal service, the new service could be run by the Secretary of State. This would ensure a minimum standard of competence and independence from the local authorities. Others believed that this would cut at the roots of the community council idea because it would be placing responsibility for a big part of the system as far away from the community as could be imagined. They felt that if such a national service were to exist, its control should lie with a consortium of community councils formed, probably, by groupings at regional level. Neither solution is ideal but discussion of them at least helps to show that the post of secretary is a crucial one and should not be left unconsidered during discussion of district council schemes.

Before leaving this chapter one other issue must be discussed: the extent to which the local authorities themselves might provide the services required by the community councils. In theory, there is no reason why a local authority should not provide accommodation, clerical, duplicating and secretarial services to the community councils in its area. There are plenty of precedents for such action. The part-time secretary of a local community council might be an administrative officer of the local authority who would be expected to act independently while serving in that capacity. After all, the secretary of a Royal Commission is nearly always a career civil servant who is nevertheless expected to serve the commission faithfully no matter how critical of the government the commission wishes to be. And since the main purpose of a community council is to make as effective as possible communication between the local authority and the local community what better method would be found than to have a servant of the former the secretary of the latter? Tempting it may be, acceptable it is not. Even if the local authority officer observed most scrupulously the independence of his community council the suspicion would almost certainly arise that he was not doing so. Each time a community protest was ineffective in changing a local authority policy, or some policy decision slipped by unremarked until too late, the community would feel that it had not been energetically enough served by someone who is, after all, one of 'them'. The position may be slightly different in the case of a local authority community worker since such double loyalties are intrinsic to his work and there are many examples of local authority employees working effectively to arouse a local community to do battle with their employing authority. In the early stages of community councils some may need the kind of skilled help which a community worker can give, but such help should be as short-term as possible. It is notoriously hard for anyone to serve two masters and it is neither fair nor desirable to put a local authority employee in the position where loyal service to one master is liable to jeopardize his position with the other.

It is an important principle of community work that the 'client community' should be helped to look after itself as rapidly as possible and a community which cannot find one of its own members to act as secretary to the community council after a few meetings is almost certainly unready to use one effectively.

Accommodation and other services are in a different category and there is no strong reason (save perhaps the presentational one that it looks better if an independent body meets on independent ground) why the local authority should not provide them. Even so, there is much to be said for the local authority providing grants in cash rather than in kind since to do so allows the community council a choice. There are, after all, a growing number of voluntary bodies which operate cheap duplicating and other services and a community council might well prefer to shop around for the best bargain than be constrained by the nature of the grant arrangements to use the local authority's services at times dictated by the local authority.

Summary

This chapter has been concerned with the functions of a community council and with a possible structure for performing them. It accepts the necessity of linking the community councils to recognizable geographical boundaries but stresses the inadequacy of a geographical base by itself. Community of interest matters more than fortuitous physical propinquity as a foundation of effective co-operation and any structure we create must make it possible for interest-based groupings to emerge rapidly and on a broad base. Independence from the local authority and as wide a membership as possible are essential to a council's prosperity and, as far as can be achieved, management by an élite—however created—should be avoided. These are difficult aims but if the plenary public session is recognized as the centre of all power and authority in the community council they may not prove unattainable.

Notes

1. Ruth Beard, Contribution to a seminar at Edinburgh University on teaching methods.

2. N. Burnet, 'Access for the Disabled: A Project in Levenmouth' (*Focus*, February 1972).

3. Paul Harrison, 'The Neighbourhood Council' (*New Society* 12 April 1973).

4. cp. Circular No. 1972/39 of the District Councils' Association.

5. The argument that without powers the community councils will be ineffective is discussed in Chapter 7 where the parallel with parish councils is examined.

6. cp. J. J. Rousseau, *Social Contract*. O.U.P. 1971.

7. See, for example, the tentative groupings suggested by existing district councils in East Lothian.

8. This is, of course, well known to community workers and a good example of this is to be found in the Edinburgh Council of Social Service's experience of community work in Edinburgh.

9. The list of volunteers prepared to serve on Children's Hearings are known as Children's Panels and these have already begun to form into associations for both improving their own performance and for bringing pressure to bear on central and local government for improved facilities.

10. There is copious literature to show the unrepresentative nature of the active membership of voluntary organizations. See also, as contrasting types of activity which show the same characteristic also, (a) the composition of children's panels in Scotland; (b) the composition of boards of trustees of charitable trusts.

11. See, for example, the amendments submitted by the Scottish Council of Social Service on the Local Government (Scotland) Bill, April 1973.

12. Paul Harrison, 'The Neighbourhood Council' (*New Society* 12 April 1973).

13. Scottish Development Department Circular, 'Community Councils'. L/LGR/48, 2 August 1972.

14. Public prosecutors under Scots law.

3

Community Councils
and the National Health Service

We now come to one of the less justifiable developments provided for under the Act: the creation of local health councils
(community health councils in England).

Successive governments have been so unable or unwilling to
experiment with new ways of financing local government that
it was inevitable that when the N.H.S. was reorganized it would
remain separate, cut off simultaneously from democratic control
and from all the other social services whose links with it are
recognized more clearly every year. Even Sir Keith Joseph[1]
was reduced to defending the decision on such weak philosophical ground that most spokesmen have preferred to dwell
upon the practical ones of expense or the strength of the medical
lobby. At the same time it was recognized that there should be
within the service 'a voice for the local public'.

One obvious means of achieving this aim, given that the
Government had no intention of allowing the National Health
Service management to fall into the hands of people elected by
their fellow citizens, would have been to establish local health
councils democratically elected by voters in their own locality.
This would have perpetuated the élitist tradition, but would at
least have had the merit of being both traditional and widely
understood.

An alternative, which would have been available in Scotland
and which was, indeed, contemplated at one stage,[2] would have
been to have given the function to the new community councils.
What could hardly have been foreseen was that both in England
and Wales and in Scotland, the aim of representing the consumer
and of ensuring that what the Scottish consultative document[3]
calls 'positive public participation and support' was to be sought
by a system of *appointment*. Some of the members are to be
appointed, admittedly on the nomination of local voluntary

organizations, by the Area Health Boards, which, as we have already seen, are far from representative of the community at large, and the fears of Mr John Smith, M.P., speaking in the Standing Committee Debate[4] on the Bill seem only too likely to be justified. He said

> I should have thought that there would be an inevitable tendency for Health Board members not to encourage members of a health council who would be expected to be critical of them. They would no doubt describe their operation as going for responsible members of the community, but sometimes the description 'responsible' is just another name for 'ineffective, unwilling to criticize actively'.

The rest of the members are to be appointed by the local authorities within the area of the Health Board. There are to be no restrictions upon their choice, but we are bound to ask whether an active and critical individual, well known to the local people in a small locality is likely to gain the appointment in competition with more 'respectable' figures whose activities hitherto may not have made him well known to the community so much as to the elected members and the officials of the local authority. In other words, which will be the determinant of the choice, the wishes of the community or the predilections of the elected representatives? It may be argued that the latter's view of the National Health Service is likely to be more 'responsible' than that of members of the public who have not had their experience of being responsible for a service, but it is the consumer's voice which is being sought, not the opinions of people likely to take a managerial view.

What we have, therefore, is an undemocratically appointed management clique being watched over and assisted by another appointed group which is almost certain to turn into a very similar clique. Indeed, the Scottish Under-Secretary of State in the Conservative Government has publicly said that he looks forward to a time when, 'once the health councils have been set up, they will be able to make known their views on future appointments. They will be able to say whether they are getting members who are critical both constructively and negatively.'[5] And, presumably, help to shape the clique which comes after them.

In an attempt to introduce at least a semblance of democracy into this process a study group in East Sussex under the chairmanship of Dr P. J. M. McEwan[6] recommended that the representation of the voluntary organizations should be achieved by asking all voluntary organizations within the community each to nominate a representative and then holding an election in which each of the nominating organizations should have a vote. This does nothing to reduce the disadvantage that the resulting group is still likely to turn into an élite, but does at least ensure that it is the voluntary organizations themselves and not the Health Board who have the final say.

Let us look a little more closely at the intended functions of these councils. In general, as we have seen, they are to 'fulfil the essential task of representing the views of the local community and provide an effective "consumer" voice'. Among the interests which they are expected to have in the discharge of these functions are listed the following:

1   They are to express the community view on the general quality of the services being provided in the district and their adequacy in relation to health care needs. (The Health Board is to provide the necessary statistical and other information.)
2   To examine and comment constructively upon the Health Board's plans for the provision and development of services. 'Councils will be entitled to be consulted by Health Boards about future plans and intentions' but are also expected to take the initiative.
3   Changes in services.
4   Facilities for patients, including such matters as visiting arrangements, waiting times, etc.
5   Waiting lists.
6   Quality of services, such as laundry, catering, etc. (no mention of nursing, doctoring, etc.).
7   Volume and type of complaints, although the investigation of individual complaints is to be for management.

We have only to look at this list to see the enormity of the intention to keep the local health councils separate from the community councils. The first one—'the general quality of the services being provided in the district and their adequacy in relation to health care needs'—cannot be appreciated without an understanding of the district as a whole and of the communities within it. It will clearly be a Health Board responsibility to decide the number of geriatric beds needed within the district, for example, but if community participation means anything it must mean that the decision can only be taken after the local community has had a chance to discuss the extent to which it intends to develop voluntary visiting and caring services, old people's clubs, statutory and voluntary arrangements for receiving old people back from hospital, etc. The travelling arrangements available to the dependents of old people, and indeed the whole nature of the local communities, all have a bearing on the need for admission to hospital.[7] Yet the Government seems quite happy to compound the difficulties created by the separate administration of the social work and health services by deliberately separating these community concerns from the new machinery specially devised to communicate community wisdom and opinion to the local authorities and other bodies.

Similar considerations apply to almost all of the suggested functions. 'The range of services provided at health centres', 'visiting arrangements', 'closures of hospitals', all these affect the community as a whole and not just that part of it which happens, by an arbitrary act of administrative choice, to be regarded as peculiarly interested in health care. If a bus service is curtailed, the local hospital's visiting hours may have to be altered; if a local hospital is closed, the bus service may need to take account of the travelling forced upon people by the transfer of the hospital's services to another place. It can hardly be sensible for a health board to try to reach conclusions about whether it is more economical for the public to travel to a consultant or for him to do the travelling unless it has taken fully into account the local community's attitudes towards the centre wherein the visiting consultancy might take place. And the community's attitudes may have more to do with such phenomena as early closing day or the proximity of the school than with considerations exclusively of health.

Moreover, if the community councils were to succeed in fostering an effective sense of community self-awareness and confidence; if they genuinely released a flow of helpful advice and suggestion, as well as criticism and complaint, what is the justification for keeping the health service out of it? To do so is merely to demonstrate once again that tendency to compartment whole people into convenient administrative categories, which is the bane of so much of our policy making. If there are serious catering difficulties in the local hospital it is conceivable that a member of the local community who has worked in a school meals service, or catered for a passenger liner or simply travelled widely and used a wide variety of different catering facilities, has something valuable to offer. Such a person is unlikely even to hear of the problem if it is aired only in a health service setting, among people chosen principally because of their interest in health services. It would have been very much more satisfactory if community participation in health service organization had been treated in the same way as participation in housing, education, social work or any of the other aspects of policy making which so closely affect it.

A strong argument in favour of combining the two channels of community opinion was made by Sir John Brotherston at a conference in Edinburgh organized by the Scottish Council of Social Service. Sir John pointed out that the three major groups of crippling or fatal disease in Scotland are those associated with alcohol, respiratory diseases affected by smoking and diseases associated with over-eating. In the past, the Health Service has been brought in to cope with these perils only after the damage has been done and all that can be done is an attempt to salvage something from the wreckage. If society is to make any effective assault upon these diseases it must be done through social pressure brought to bear through a massive change in public attitudes. In such an endeavour, it is the community councils rather than the health councils which ought to be involved.

Before we pass on to discover if anything can be salvaged from this lamentable decision, it is worth pausing briefly to look at how it was taken. As we have noted, there was originally in the Scottish White Paper a suggestion that the proposed community councils might be the means for assuring the public of a voice in the planning of the Health Service. How did it get lost? One major difficulty was obviously that of timing. The reorganization of the Health Service preceded that of local government. This produced its embarrassments for the Government over the proposed Area Health Board boundaries designed to coincide with the boundaries of local government areas not yet agreed. As Sir John Gilmour, M.P. for East Fife, never tired of pointing out, decisions about the organization of the Health Service could not be allowed to predetermine the fate of areas such as his (which he was, of course, destined to see drastically changed from the original intention). A second difficulty seems to have been that it was seen as essential to include some semblance of community participation in the National Health Service Bill, and it could not be left too vague or it would not satisfy those who, like Barbara Castle, regarded as 'totally inadequate the injection of democracy into the Health Service'.[8] It seems probable that, confronted with the need to define reasonably specifically the nature of the local health councils and confronted by a marked reluctance on the part of those responsible for drafting the local government legislation to define anything at all about community councils,[9] the draftsmen felt bound to go for their own scheme. No doubt, too, the influence of England and Wales and of Northern Ireland made itself felt, since, after all, the links between Scottish Home and Health Department (S.H.H.D.) and Department of Health and Social Security are almost as close as (and in some respects closer than) those between Scottish Home and Health Department and Scottish Development Department. Nevertheless, as we have seen, the preference of the Minister, even as late as the Standing Committee debate, was for a form of words which would allow any area that wished to do so to rely upon the community council to perform the health council's function. In a remarkable act of generosity (or was it merely a declaration of the unimportance of the whole matter?), Mr Munro allowed the opposition to choose whether to insist on a separate health council in each area or to leave in the enabling clause[10] which would allow them to have one but would not force one upon them.[11] They chose the mandatory wording but it is ironic that in their zeal to ensure that no Area Health Board should be allowed to evade its obligations to consult the public, the very spokesmen who had been most critical of the absence of proper democratic procedures in the National Health Service should have chosen to destroy one of the remaining opportunities to introduce them.

If we accept that there is nothing at this stage that can be done to upset the principle, what benefits can community councils obtain from a study of the proposed health councils? There are several. First, it is clear that the Secretary of State intended that they should be as effective as possible. The consultative document stated that, 'it is the Secretary of State's intention to ... give local health councils *information and authority* [my italics] to ensure their effective working'. It would be admirable if the Secretary of State were prepared to interest himself to the same extent in community councils. It will be argued that because the latter are a part of local government the Secretary of State cannot interfere, but there is no reason why he should not produce some firm guidance as to the kind of information which should be made available by local authorities to community councils.

Second, it is obvious that the Secretary of State intends the health councils to be reasonably well financed. In the present proposals it is suggested that the council's secretary should be 'an experienced N.H.S. officer within a few years of retirement'[12] or someone of similar seniority from elsewhere. Dr McEwan's study group has suggested that the secretary should have a minimum salary of £3,000-£4,000 per annum and, as Draper and Smart[13] point out, a council staffed on that level will require a budget of at least £10,000 per annum.

There are obvious disadvantages, as well as equally obvious benefits, attached to employing as chief executive someone as steeped in the Health Service traditions and modes of thought as this advice implies. The Edinburgh conference was certainly far from enthusiastic about it. Consideration should rather be given to the suggestion that a bright and energetic outsider can usually learn quickly enough to be useful without necessarily blunting all the critical faculties with which an outsider can often approach an organization. Nevertheless, it is encouraging to see that in the Health Service the intention is to provide a proper administrative support to the health councils. One has only to remember how much larger the budget of the local authorities is than that of the Health Service to show that the currently widespread suggestions that community councils can be run on the cheap are inadmissible.[14]

It is unfortunate that the intention is for the Area Health Board to finance the councils entirely since, 'people seldom cherish a dog which consistently bites the hand that feeds it',[15] but we must hope that the councils will speedily create for themselves within the community the kind of position which would make it almost impossible for the Health Board to starve them.

A last feature of the proposals which seems valuable for the community councils is the suggestion that the Health Boards should arrange to hold a meeting at least once a year with all the local health councils in its area 'to consider how far the objectives of the service have been attained and to outline the general intentions for the future'. Local authorities might profitably do the same with the community councils in their area, although preferably with a rather more equal balance between giving and receiving information. (In this connection it is also helpful to note that the emergence of a national association is foreseen.)

At the time of writing there seems to be one possibility for repairing some of the damage caused by removing from the community councils such an important and emotive topic as health. Under the Act there is no reason why the members who are to be nominated by the local authority to the local health council should not be nominated, at least for some of their number, by the community councils in the area grouped as necessary for the purpose. At least, in this way, some unfamiliar faces might be seen on the councils and some unusual opinions voiced. Moreover, some firm connection between the two types of council could be thus established.

Yet, when all is said, it is bitterly disappointing that such a traditionally élitist and separatist body should be the only concession to democracy in the reorganized Health Service.

Notes

1. See, for example, Sir Keith Joseph: 'There are so many competing needs for taxpayers' money that if we filled the area health authorities with people who had allegiance to another body they would not be as free as we wish to make a decision between the competing

needs.' Statement to the House of Commons, August 1972. He was, of course, talking about a service whose links with other services are only too often obscured by its administrative separation from them.

2. See the White Paper and *Hansard*, 13 June 1972, N.H.S. (Scotland) Bill, First Scottish Standing Committee.
3. Reorganization of the Scottish Health Service, Local Health Councils.
4. First Scottish Standing Committee, N.H.S. (Scotland) Bill, 13 June 1972, Col. 246.
5. Mr Hector Monro. Debate of First Scottish Standing Committee, 13 June 1972. *Hansard* Col. 249.
6. Area 44 Health Services Project (East Sussex). Report by Second Phase Advisory Group: 'The Consumer and the Health Service'.
7. See P. Townsend, *Last Refuge*, especially Chapter 9 'Reasons for Admission'. Routledge and Kegan Paul 1964.
8 *Hansard*, Vol. 842, Col. 350, 1 August 1972.
9. For an example of this reluctance see the Scottish Development Department (S.D.D.) circular of 2 August 1972.
10. See *Hansard*, First Scottish Standing Committee debate, Col. 242, 13 June 1972.
11. Reorganization of the Scottish Health Service. Cmnd 4734, Paragraph 11. 'Alternatively the functions of these councils [in bringing together representatives of the local committee without executive responsibilities (and therefore uncommitted to local management policies) but with a keen and constructive interest in their local services] might be performed by the community councils discussed in the White Paper on Local Government Reform.'
12. A proposal which met with sharp disappointment from the members of a conference held at Edinburgh University to discuss the document. The argument was that the Councils would have difficulty enough in avoiding being dominated by N.H.S. views without having an N.H.S. secretary.
13. P. Draper and T. Smart, N.H.S. Reorganization Project, Department of Community Medicine, Guy's Hospital Medical School.
14. See Chapter 4 on Finance.
15. Sir William Murrie discussing the Council on Tribunals.

4

Finance

The question of how the community councils should be financed
and of how much they should receive is as basic to ask as it is
hard to answer. If we look first at how much they are likely to
need we walk straight into a tangle of conflicting priorities and
principles dense enough to daunt the boldest speculator. Nevertheless, we must attempt to define the problems if we are to
come near suggesting any answers.

Among the strands in our tangle are

1 Huge variations between areas,
2 Periodic variations in community council activity,
3 Wide differences in the operations of local authority
  themselves.

Let us take these in turn:

1 *Huge variations between areas*

However the district council schemes finally turn out, it seems
inevitable that community council areas will vary in size of
population, acreage, rateable value, age composition, etc. even
more than the district council areas themselves. They will also
vary widely in less tangible attributes such as self-confidence
and public interest. This at once implies that what would be a
reasonable support grant for one area would be wholly inadequate for another. It was mainly for this reason that the
Government rejected an amendment to the Local Government
Bill designed to secure a *per capita* levy on the rates. They
did not, however, suggest any alternative source of public finance
beyond the entirely discretionary grant from the district and
regional councils envisaged in the first draft of the legislation.

2 *Periodic variations in community council activity*

It is virtually certain that even if community councils are claimed by every eligible area their operation will vary widely, depending particularly upon the supply of locally important issues. We have already seen (Chapter 2) that it is reasonable to expect community participation to proceed in spurts of enthusiasm when a particular problem excites local interest, followed by periods of comparative inertia in which the community is willing to leave its affairs in the hands of its elected representatives. Although it would obviously be possible to allow a community council to bank its income against the day when it wished to burst into life anew, it would be against traditional practice and it seems more promising to try to evolve a system of financing flexible enough to be able to respond to changes in the level of community council activity as they occur.

3 *Differences in the operations of local authorities*

It is obvious that local authorities (and other bodies such as area health boards and nationalized industries) will differ widely in the amount of positive encouragement they give to public participation and, since it is they who will mostly be responsible for producing plans, their behaviour will directly affect that of the community councils. In the debate on the sections of the Bill devoted to community councils the Government spokesman refused to give community councils any statutory right to be consulted. This was because of the difficulty of drafting adequate powers, because it was thought restrictive to single out one possible community function for statutory definition and because experience suggested that 'the requirement to consult with respect to legislation, to provide information in advance, sometimes make the body concerned as determined as possible to observe it to the *minimum* legal extent . . .'[1] The safeguard for the community councils, the Government suggested, lay not in statutory powers, but in building themselves into a position where they could demand to be consulted, reinforcing their importunity with the media and other channels of public communication. Such activity involves public education through exhibitions, public meetings, advertisement, as well as time freely given by the media because of the activity's news value. It costs money and if the local authority in an area is unwilling to make it easy for a community council to obtain information, it will cause the community council more expense.

The converse may also be true. A local authority which is exemplary in its willingness to consult the community may also cause the community council considerable expense simply by enlarging the number of occasions upon which consultation is possible. As I have quoted elsewhere,[2] the London Borough of Camden spent a minimum of £17,500 on consulting its residents upon the long-term plan for the area and that was only one exercise, albeit an important one.

This brings us to the second set of questions: who shall be responsible for providing the money required by community councils? The Bill is quite clear: 'Regional, islands and district councils may make such contributions as they think fit towards the expenses of community councils within their areas ...'[3] Finance, in other words, at the discretion of the local authorities themselves. The legislation, of course, allows the councils to seek other means of finance such as public subscription and charitable giving. It will be interesting to see if community councils will be allowed to run regular lotteries—a form of self-financing which might go some way towards equalizing financial resources between areas! The evidence of the ninth district council of Lanark to the Wheatley commission suggested that members of community councils be asked to pay a minimal subscription but, while the idea has merit in that what people pay for they tend to value, the possibility of some poorer or younger members being thus excluded is not to be lightly ignored.

Public subscription may well prove a reasonable way of meeting exceptional expenses (such as a major protest) but it is clear that the government is right to expect that the major finance will come from the local authorities. The objections to this are obvious enough and were well stated during the passage of the Bill.[4] They include the danger that a local authority will be reluctant to finance a body which is effectively kicking them and that a local authority which disagrees with the particular line taken by a community council on one issue will allow that disagreement to colour the discussion of grant aid for the other functions of the community council. This danger can be exaggerated. If a community council suceeds in earning a reputation for itself as an effective body with a wide base within the community the local authorities will hardly dare to starve it of funds. There are good examples of voluntary organizations (particularly in the amenity field) gaining a position where the local authority feels bound to try to gain their approval or at least their acquiescence in the policy-making game. Nevertheless, the dangers are there for all to see. It will often be those community councils which are least experienced in influencing decisions which will arouse local authority antagonism by their tactics or their views, and if the consequence is a diminution of their resources they will never succeed in establishing the kind of position which a more experienced (probably middle-class) community will win for itself comparatively early. A further difficulty is that the local authorities may find themselves in a genuine dilemma over how best to foster community councils. In areas where the local authority appears keener than the community to create good consultative machinery it will be tempting for the authority to provide help in kind rather than in cash. If the community worker, or the secretary of the community council, is paid for directly out of the local authority's budget it is easier for the authority to ensure that standards are achieved which seem acceptable to it. Such benevolent paternalism is creditable enough to the local authority, but is likely to mute the community's responses and will, to that extent, reduce the chances of the emergence of an effective community council.

Moreover, nothing in the proposals so far goes any way towards meeting the objection that some areas not only start off better equipped to make their community councils effective, but will have the financial resources to consolidate their lead. I have argued above that it would be folly to bowdlerize community participation for the sake of achieving paternalist redistribution of resources, but we cannot afford to ignore the dangers inherent in a situation where the already affluent areas are provided with a powerful statutory opportunity to retain their privileged position.

What we want, therefore, is a method of financing community councils which will

1   Effect some redistribution of resources in favour of the deprived communities,
2   Ensure that a realistic sum is spent on them,
3   Safeguard their independence and retain the virtually unlimited opportunities given to them by the Act.
    (G. Younger)[5]

And all this has to be achieved within the present statutory provisions.

Redistribution

If the poorer areas are to be given extra resources to allow them to compete (at least in part) with the richer ones, how will the criteria for additional aid be established, who will establish them and who will find the money? Let us assume, for a moment, that every locality defined under the district council scheme has decided to establish a community council. Let us also assume that a district of 40,000 inhabitants has decided on a scheme which defines a community council area for every 5,000 inhabitants on average. In this district, therefore, there will be eight community councils. For the moment we shall ignore the form of constitution adopted by the councils, beyond remarking hopefully that this district has not insisted on one common constitution for every council in the district. One need is common to them all, however: secretarial services. No matter how low the preferred level of activity, someone has to be the correspondent of the community council; the material from local authorities and elsewhere has to go through somebody's letterbox.

Some of the community councils in our district are rich and some are poor, but at this low level they all have the same need. How shall it be provided? The choices before the district council are many, but they include the following:

a   The district council provides one or more officers to serve for part of his or her time as secretary to the community councils. If the work increases, the district council provides increased officer time. This is redistributive to a small degree since the higher rates of the richer areas buy them no more service than those of the poorer. At least in theory this seems to secure our purpose even if we have reservations (see Chapter 2) about the secretary of a community council being also an officer of the local authority.

Yet the appearance of redistribution could easily be illusory. If the richer areas turn out to be also the more self-confident ones from the beginning, they will generate more work than the less confident ones so that, with the best of intentions, the secretary will find himself devoting more time to the demanding councils in terms of minutes, notices of meetings, preparation of documents, etc.

Moreover, in this situation, who decides whether the preoccupations of the richer areas are more or less important than those of the poorer? If the bulk of the secretarial resources are provided directly by the district council it could happen that more time and money are spent upon the peripheral anxieties of the rich than upon the central concerns of the poor.

b The district council could provide money which each community council could spend as it wished: on secretary, newsletter, premises, surveys, etc.

This provides more independence for the community council and helps to ensure that demand is generated properly from below, but it does not answer the question: how does the district council decide when a community council is entitled to extra help?

Any suggestion that criteria similar to those used for equalizing the rate support grant, e.g. miles of road, age of population, etc., presupposes that we can predict reasonably accurately what will stimulate community council activity. It would, in theory, be possible to create a list of activities such as the creation of a major plan, the decision to close a service centre such as a school, etc. but it would be a brave man who claimed that we know enough at present to make such an attempt remotely convincing.

It is, moreover, reasonable to assume that the eight

community councils in our district will, between them, generate more demands for financial assistance than the district (or regional) council is prepared to meet. (I know that the reverse was true of the former district councils, who seldom precepted upon the rates for the full amount of their entitlement, but their duties were commonly regarded as so petty that only a handful of districts were prepared to exercise real imagination in carrying them out to the limit of their financial capacity. For the sake of this discussion we must assume that the community councils are reasonably active throughout the country.) In that case, will it be a matter of first come, first served, in which case the more experienced areas are likely to be more successful, at least at first, in hurrying their proposals through to the grant-giving authority? If not, will it depend on the district or regional council to decide between proposals? If so, we are immediately back in the dilemma that the community councils are dependent upon the approval of the very bodies they may wish to criticize for the resources necessary to prepare their criticism.

c   A third possibility open to the local authorities would be to declare each year the maximum figure which they propose to spend upon grant aiding community councils and deposit it in a fund administered by a group of independent 'trustees'. These might be appointed by the community councils themselves (in the district we are imagining the number would be only a manageable group of eight if there were one 'trustee' for each community council area). This group would be confronted by exactly the same problems in distributing the available money as the local authorities would have been, but they would, however, be seen to be independent, and might well favour bolder experiments and more critical approaches than the local authorities, whose accountability to party organizations, traditionally more sensitive to orthodox pressure groups than to the voice of the 'silent majority', might inhibit them. It would be necessary for the 'trustees' to define (or have defined for them in the district council scheme, which will have to be submitted for approval to the Secretary of State) a minimum entitlement to which every community council would have a right, even if in some years they did not all claim it. In other words, even if a community council lay dormant for eleven months in one financial year, the local community would know that if they sprang into life in the twelfth month there would still be a minimum sum lying to their account in the trustees' fund.

It would be possible for the 'trustees' to work out their own rules for financing councils and they would be expected to justify the rules at the meetings of the local community councils at which the 'trustees' for the coming year would be appointed. Great flexibility could be observed in the making of the rules so as to secure redistribution and it would be possible for the 'trustees' to introduce, for example, a kind of matching contribution scheme in reverse so that areas with low rating yields, which raised a certain sum for themselves, could have it matched at double or treble the rate given to areas with high rating yields. This system would be able theoretically to achieve both some degree of redistribution and a considerable degree of independence for community councils—at least from the local authorities if not from each other. It would, in fact, strengthen the potential bonds between the community councils, since representatives appointed by each council would be meeting regularly and an exchange of information would be bound to result.[6] If it is objected that the trustees would form an élite of the kind I have been anxious to avoid, I reply that not only would the 'trustees' be up for election annually after a session at which they would be expected to explain their record to the community but also that they would not hold any position of authority in the structure of their own community council.

The 'trust' fund idea also allows regional and district councils freedom to grant aid directly any community council project of special interest and value to them over and above their contribution to the trust fund. It also gets round the problem that some community councils will be active only spasmodically, since within the predictable figure entered in the local authority's budget as a total expenditure for the year, the trustees will be free to allocate resources according to the level of local community council activities. It also ensures that the allocation within the budget is free of party politics and not subject to the political vagaries of the councils.

The idea of a community trust is hardly new and there are examples in the U.S.A. and Canada as well as in Britain to be called on.[7] In Scotland it would certainly be possible, if it were desired, to include in the trust common good funds and other local resources although care would obviously be needed to see that, where the boundaries of the new trust area did not coincide with those of the old funds' areas, arrangements satisfactory to the local people were written into the new community trust deed. In some areas, at least, the new fund might be expected to attract new philanthropic funds although in most areas the largest single contribution would presumably be from the local authorities.

There is one other problem which the 'trustees' would need to face with the local authorities. If, as I believe is indispensable to the success of community councils, central offices at national and/or regional level are established, who pays for them? One possibility is that the local 'trust' funds subscribe either as they see fit or according to rules made jointly by the local authorities and the community councils. Starter finance might well be required from central government or from a local government pool, but thereafter it would be at least theoretically possible to charge fees for services (cf. the charges made to local Citizens' Advice Bureaux for Citizen's Advice News Sheet) in order to keep afloat the central organization. This would allow local districts to choose for themselves what size of contribution they cared to make to the central organization. The latter would also be free to approach charitable trusts and other sources of extra finance.

None of this, however, answers my third question: how do we ensure that the local authorities contribute enough to the community councils? First of all, it would be helpful to be able to forecast what a typical community council would spend in a year, but as we have seen there will be no such creature as a typical community council. In one locality the community council may be concentrating on the sort of issues which concern many of the neighbourhood councils currently in existence, e.g. the collection of rubbish from the streets, local vandalism, play schemes for the children, etc., while another may be contributing enormously to a joint endeavour with the local authority to press for an improved ferry service or the creation of a major structural plan designed to help the local communities cope with the repercussions of oil development, oceanspan, or the siting of a new airport.

Neither can we foresee a typical local authority response. In some areas, no doubt, the traditional attitude that (even in the face of electoral apathy and growing official secrecy about long-term plans) the elected councillor must remain the proper channel for all community participation, will mean that the regional and district councils will make little or grudging use of the community councils in their area and will see their likely expenditure in the same terms as the Northern Irish consultative group saw that of the ward councils which they hoped to see established following the report of the MacRory Commission.[8] That is, about £100-£250 per annum with other expenses, such as premises, being absorbed in the ordinary budgets of the local authorities. In other areas, it is as conceivable as it is to be hoped, that the local authorities will turn increasingly to the community councils in their areas as partners in the process of collecting and disseminating information and in the policy making based thereon.

Another problem is that it will be difficult for local authorities to make a meaningful allocation of funds based on population figures. Rating yields, too, are little help by themselves, not only because the poorer areas need more help than the richer ones, but also because there is no reason to suppose that the expenditure of community councils will bear any relation to the size of the population covered by them. In the Island of Lewis, for example (pop. 15,000 approx.), where the Council of Social Service is an active body already involving fishing organizations and farming groups and many other interests, it seems likely that the contribution of the community council to the local authority's plan making will be out of all proportion to the size of the population. The opposite might be true in densely populated urban areas, at least at first. In such areas with reasonably easy informal communication and a host of vexatious but comparatively small scale problems the community councils may decide to spend most of their time on activities which require less expensive support. Against this, however, we must remember that in towns the need for several community councils to combine to tackle some large common problem may exceed that in rural areas. It may happen, therefore, that local community councils will wish to contribute substantially towards the cost of maintaining an effective central office.

Yet if we cannot hope to find a 'typical' community council nor a 'typical' local authority some estimates can be attempted and it will be a clear indication of how serious the government is in its desire to foster community councils, whether the local authorities are encouraged to pitch their estimates high or low.

The community development projects, urban aid grants, and voluntary endeavours, such as the S.N.A.P. have all shown how much money can be used before a community begins to make an impact upon the plan makers. Even in a tiny project, the voluntary organizations committee project of the Edinburgh Council of Social Service (V.O.C.), the sums required dwarfed the suggestions often heard that two or three hundred pounds towards the stationery and telephone bill of a part-time voluntary secretary will be sufficient. In order to provide an effective central pivot for the exchange of information and the creation of joint policy making opportunities for some ninety voluntary bodies in the city of Edinburgh, a charitable trust provided starting finance of £6,300 per annum for three years. In addition to this, the Council of Social Service provided the accommodation, shared the costs of duplicating and, later, photolithography machinery, and has helped the Committee to find additional finance for special projects. Experience shows that keeping moving a joint consultation on, say, the provision of adequate housing for old people in an area or the creation of adequate recreational facilities, requires many hours of secretarial time. Unless the secretary is in a position to give the work a proper degree of priority the consultative group of volunteers meets at intervals so long apart that momentum is lost, interest diminished and, most dangerous of all, either pressure on the statutory authorities is relaxed or crucial official planning deadlines are missed and the effectiveness of the venture is destroyed. Full-time staff is, therefore, essential to provide the continuous underpinning upon which voluntary endeavour can thrive. Whether every community council needs full-time professional support remains to be discovered when the system has begun to operate and, once again, the balance between providing each local community with the resources to employ community council staff for themselves and providing staff to a central agency controlled by the community councils as a whole and common to all of them is a tricky one.

Perhaps some policy such as the following should be adopted at the outset and modified in the light of experience.

Each region and district council should state that it will be prepared to spend *not less* than one per cent of its budget upon community councils. The local authorities will divide this sum between the community councils in their areas upon request but in the hope that the community councils in each district will rapidly come together to make general policy for community councils in the district. It may well be that such joint meeting will result in the creation of a central community council office charged with functions like those discussed in Chapter 2 above. In that case, the community councils will also be able to determine how they would like this central resource to be financed: by levy, on a fee-for-service basis, or a grant direct by the local authorities (which would be likely to mean a reduction in the amount of subsidy available to each local council). If, in addition, the idea of an independently administered community council fund was accepted, this would be established within the first year and thereafter the local authorities would pay their money to the 'trustees'. The Appendix shows what one per cent of the budget would mean for regions.

It is important to stress that this one per cent would be a minimum figure, although the local authorities at the beginning would be allowed to reduce the sum available in the second year by the amount unspent in the first in order to allow for a slow start to the system.

So far I have said nothing about another major source of expense which many believe to be indispensable to the success of community councils: the employment of community workers. This is as tricky as it is important. So far, the use of community workers in Britain has been as varied in its appearance as in its usefulness. Some are employed by local authorities, often by two or more departments within one authority.

Some are employed by voluntary organizations: councils of social service, for example, and have usually localized but fairly general terms of reference. Others again may be part of a special project team financed by either central government—community development projects and the like—or by voluntary organizations with a particular philosophy to try out, e.g. S.N.A.P.

Some community workers manage to achieve a position where they appear genuinely answerable only to the community among whom they work, but it is comparatively seldom that a community manages to employ its own development officer on terms of reference established by the community itself.

In a field so varied, so shifting and so little documented it is rash to try to derive any general lessons from experience since almost any generalization could no doubt be undermined by a particular local experience. Nevertheless, some may perhaps be hazarded. First, community development workers believe that true community work must start 'at the grass roots', that it must grow from involvement with local people at the most basic, house to house level. Second, they believe that the job of the community worker is to enable a local community (and definitions of a community are as elusive among community workers as they are among anyone else) to express its own aspirations and preferences and not those of the community worker. Third, they are concerned mainly with the powerless and the deprived. Most community workers are employed in areas where multiple disadvantages combine to render the local inhabitants even more ineffective *vis-à-vis* the local authority and other power structures than people elsewhere. For most, if not all, community workers a mainspring of their activity is the desire to tip the balance, at least fractionally, away from the traditionally self-assured and prosperous towards the disadvantaged. One can only agree with these aims and applaud the dedication and often astonishing success with which community development workers (under a wide variety of confusing titles) pursue them in deprived areas all over Britain. Yet one is also bound to ask: how successful are they in the long term? Have they really achieved any noticeable change in the distribution of power within the political system? To an outsider, the pattern of much community work is depressingly familiar. A community worker, professional or voluntary, arrives in an area of multiple problems, seizes almost at once upon some issue of burning local concern and begins to canalize the strong local feeling about it into a vigorous assembly of local people. Under the worker's unobtrusive (or sometimes evangelical) guidance meetings are held, practical work is undertaken, protests are organized, services started and an encouraging degree of self-confidence fostered within the community. The mothers who have been helped first to form and then to run the local playgroup learn how to involve their husbands. They then use their new understanding of the local authority structure to press for better house maintenance, greater protection from vandalism or more recreational facilities. As their battles with the local authority intensify they confront their local councillor with increasingly tense conflicts of interest, between his loyalty to his party, his involvement with his specialist committee and his knowledge of long-term interests and plans. All these make it difficult for him to appear sufficiently partisan on behalf of the local community to satisfy the local tenants' association or neighbourhood council, which has become confident in articulating demands at a level more sophisticated than any with which the councillor has so far had to deal. If, in addition to this, the phenomenon of community participation is confined to only a handful of areas, the councillor's colleagues in the council will have little understanding of his predicament, even if they wish to have. Often, they will underestimate his difficulties or, indeed, exploit them. As a result, the effectiveness of the local councillor as an adequate channel of communication for the views of the local community begins to be questioned. Indeed, because the pressures are often centred round issues specially chosen for their wide appeal to the local inhabitants they may stimulate a short-term unity, which may well be less evident as issues arise of less common appeal, but in the meantime highlight the apparent irrelevance of the traditional political system to solve local problems. (This difficulty will grow worse under a local government system which reduces so sharply the number of councillors and which is likely to tie them even more tightly than hitherto to the round of council meetings and official duties.) At the same time, as the councillor is being 'shown' to be of little relevance, the officials too find themselves impaled on the horns of a singularly uncomfortable dilemma. Either they spend a disproportionate amount of time listening to the problems of a relatively tiny part of their total area, without coming any closer to commanding the resources to deal wth the problems, or they retire further into their shell of secrecy and closed decision making because only by reducing the amount of information available can they hope to reduce the community activity generated by its release. Thus the active community, over-encouraged by the initial response to their efforts, which may well have meant rapid execution of some overdue repairs or the doubling of the police force based on the local station, becomes increasingly disillusioned with the traditional political methods of coping with problems and turns with increasing bitterness to renewed apathy, or to tackling useful local tasks with an energy which allows them to pretend that they are still being successful, or to unconstitutional ways of protesting against the system. The latter, too, brings results for a while, but increasingly attracts the hostility of other areas as well as the irritation of the councillors for the rest of the district, so that in the end it becomes easier for the conventional politicians and officials with widespread support to ignore them. For the community worker this pattern would be hard enough to endure if it were the only problem confronting him, but there are, of course, many others. Among them is the difficulty of his own divided loyalties. Almost all workers derive their authority from their place in a recognized agency. They themselves are mostly possessors of recognized qualifications. They, therefore, often find it personally difficult to encourage activity designed to bypass the traditional patterns altogether. Moreover, they recognize, perhaps more certainly than the communities with whom they work, the necessity of allies among the establishment if the short-term goals, which are what concern the local people most, are to be realized. It is theoretically admirable to devise community structures which are almost entirely anarchist in operation and to do so may coincide exactly with the wishes both of the worker and of a small group of colleagues in the locality but as I asserted at the beginning of this book most people are not interested in politics and political structures. They want some clearly identifiable, usually short-term object, like new school classrooms before their own children leave the school or recreational facilities for teenagers before their own children marry and leave the area. Most community workers, therefore, if they follow their own code of letting the community decide its priorities for itself, find themselves bound to seek allies among the very establishment whose procedures and behaviour they so often find irrelevant or hostile. As soon as they do so, they attract to themselves a whole complex of prejudices and animosities concerned more with the nature of their allies than with the goals of the alliance. Purists will accuse them of selling out to the middle classes, or to the landlords or to the bureaucrats; the traditional enemies of their allies will immediately see them as standing in the opposing camp and will receive frostily future overtures for an alliance designed to gain a different object. Also, the choice of ally restricts the methods of operation open to the community, since some forms of behaviour will be unacceptable to some allies. Housing associations, for example, can hardly be expected to approve of rent strikes which, if later applied to them, would threaten their own existence.

A further difficulty experienced by the community worker is that his terms of reference may well be dictated by the agency which employs him and he may find that what he, as an unattached community worker, might wish to do, conflicts with them. A community worker employed to foster good race relations might find that not only was this not the burning problem in his community but that to behave as if it were would merely create problems which would make the solution of what he perceived as the real problem even harder. Similarly, community workers employed by one local authority department are almost bound to develop a list of priorities which favoured that particular department. A community worker on the staff of an education authority would be bound to interpret his job in terms of what could best be done for the young people in his community, thus wearing a pair of spectacles whose tinting might be termed distorting by a community worker attached to a different department.

The consequences of all these varied pressures seem to be that community workers follow one of three paths

1 they resign, or seek a job in another area where they believe that by starting afresh they will avoid the result which disenchanted them in their first area,

2 they seek promotion within their hierarchy and thereby confirm that they look for their fulfilment within the traditional structure,

3 they seek opportunities to destroy the traditional structure altogether and thereby, in the short-term at least, place themselves in a position where their capacity to achieve anything tangible for their clients is enormously reduced.

If this is at all a justifiable analysis, is there anything which can be done about it? Sometimes it is hard to feel optimistic in the light of all the experience which has been gained so far and both the inertia and the positive tenacity which defend the present structures, but I believe that the new system of community councils could provide us with real hope. In the first place, one of the greatest weaknesses of community work at present, the isolation and impoverishment of most of the areas where it is practised, will not need to continue. With a national system of community councils, however heterogeneous in form, aspiration and procedure, the opportunities for joint consultation, exchange of material, and indeed for sharp conflict will be legion. This should not only allow for all sorts of combined effort, but should also make it easier for community councils in one area to perceive the limitations as well as the opportunities of their own position. I am not, of course, suggesting that any consensus will emerge from such gatherings but that they will help to put an end to the parochialism which is such a feature of the present scene.[9] To agree that local community participation must concern itself with the tiny details of local life is not to say that it must do so to the exclusion of larger issues or in ignorance of the larger society around it. Secondly, the creation by statute of a national structure makes it possible for either one, or a combination of community councils, to employ, for themselves, community development officers. Indeed, it would allow for the creation of a national career structure for such workers, working not within the various compartmented agencies of our society but within a structure controlled directly by community councils. They would thus be independent of any one agency and therefore able to deal equally with all, and this with a personal position from which many of the conflicts which undermine existing community workers had been removed.

If we add the salaries of community workers to the budget for community councils we run at once into much larger sums. For the Forth region, for example, to employ a staff of community workers serving councils on a basis of one per council per 5,000 electorate, the bill would come to at least £500,000, allowing slightly less than £5,000 per community worker. Yet unless we are prepared, as a nation, to face the fact that community participation is a sophisticated ideal, difficult to handle philosophically, even harder to realize in actuality and that communities will need to have available to them a considerable amount of skilled help if they are to make it work, we might as well forget the whole enterprise. To suggest, as has been done, that if communities really want community councils the skills necessary to make them work will miraculously appear and that to make any formal help available is to introduce an undesirable degree of rigidity is claptrap. Women's Institutes have an enviable record of starting very successful branches from scratch, but they would never expect a branch to start without having assistance available. They produce published guidance, they have teams of speakers who will help new branches to learn how to run their affairs efficiently and they even run courses for intending office holders. All this is done for an activity which, astonishingly catholic though it is, covers only a fraction of what community councils might deal with. In short, whether more money is spent at the most local level or in providing central resources, the total budget for the new community councils needs to be large.

What can we hope for in return? Throughout this book I have suggested possible returns, so here I shall merely list some of them without further comment. If community councils work well I would expect results to include

1 A much wider basis for plan making than the present,
2 Much greater public interest in policy making at many levels,

3   Much better public understanding of the nature of, and
    need for, change,
4   Public services much more responsive to public opinion,
5   More self-confidence among the public, which would result
    in greater participation in other spheres such as the run-
    ning of industry or the trades unions,
6   Greater participation by the public not only in policy
    making, but also in running the affairs of their own locali-
    ties. This might well allow for a transfer of resources from
    the centralized bureaucracies to local communities and even
    for a reallocation of public resources as communities
    became active for themselves in reducing vandalism or
    providing entertainment for themselves,
7   In time, perhaps, a greater willingness to accept redistri-
    bution in favour of disadvantaged groups as greater
    understanding of the society as a whole emerged,
8   The restructuring of local government to make it much
    easier for comparatively small areas to be treated as one
    unit within the policy making machinery of local
    authorities.

If I am right, these are gains worth a considerable price. We
should hazard some finance to make them possible.

Notes

1. Lord Polwarth, Col. 1251, *Lords Hansard* No. 877.
2. *Towards Participation in Local Services.* Fabian Tract 419.
3. Local Government (Scotland) Act 1973, S.55.
4. See, for example, John Smith, M.P. First Scottish Standing Committee debate on the Local Government (Scotland) Bill. *Hansard*,
   Col. 1545, 10 April 1973. 'What is to stop a local authority from
   withholding money in the same way from a community council for
   what is agreed to be a desirable object?'
5. First Scottish Standing Committee debate. *Hansard*, Col. 1525,
   10 April 1973. 'It will be a new type of body, with a new range
   of freedom to do what it and the local people wish, unrestricted by
   statutory requirements of accountability, audit, and all the para-
   phernalia which local government has to go through.'
6. An idea which was suggested to me in another context is persuasive
   here. The Neighbourhood Projects Group in Liverpool put forward
   the idea that all the groups in the city which were competing for
   community development funds might meet together to argue out their

cases and reach their own decisions on allocation without the intervention of an arbiter. This certainly strengthens the understanding among groups but might be too hard to achieve when the activities of community councils are so varied. Nevertheless, it is an idea which could form the basis of an interesting experiment.

7. See, for example, the experiment recently established in Kelowna, British Columbia.

8. The Report of the Review Body of Local Government in Northern Ireland, 1970. H.M.S.O., Cmnd 546.

9. In this connection the requirement in the N.H.S. Act that Area Health Boards meet at least annually with their local health councils should be applied equally to community councils and district authorities.

5

Education and Community Councils

As I have suggested above the main justification for a community council must be that it draws in a genuine cross-section of the interests and activities within the community. This is not easy to do, because each group in a community tends to imagine that it, and the groups which it meets regularly, are the only ones who need to be included. I have now attended numerous meetings and conferences about community councils and it is obvious that the gathering varies according to its sponsorship. A meeting organized by an amenity association will include an entirely different selection of groups from one organized by a social welfare organization. Trades council sponsorship or Rotarian auspices will similarly bias the attendance and perhaps the only universal feature is the absence of individuals who do not belong to any organization. (This is, I believe, a further manifestation of the argument put forward on p. 35 that 'non-joiners' will only show interest in meetings concerned with matters of direct concern to themselves.) Their absence matters, however, for one reason: there will be a natural tendency for those who are already members of organizations to work to ensure that community councils are run by people like themselves and they will have a strong preference for traditional models. There is, therefore, a need for a widespread and continuing attempt to show local groups that there are other models which could be tried. The Scottish Council of Social Service is among the small handful of organizations which has so far attempted this task, but as the Council itself admits, its own role means that its links are mainly with social welfare organizations and therefore meetings under its auspices are biased in that direction. What is required is an independent organization which could easily make links with the bewildering variety of different types of body in the country and encourage local communities to set up genuinely comprehensive meetings to discuss how community councils might operate within their area. After all, the present divisions between fields of interest are being increasingly revealed as arbitrary and confusing. When a festival committee is found advising on the operation of a local health and advice centre[1] or a local history society turns into an amenity association[2] it is clear that what matters is the growth in self-confidence of a local community which allows it to speak on any issue, rather than the label 'artistic', 'recreational', 'educational' or 'social work' which at present so often serves to create artificial divisions of activity across which ideas of relevance to the whole community seldom spread.

Another point which might be made about local organizations as a basis of community council operations is that they are frequently part of their own hierarchy which is vertical rather than horizontal. It is arguable that the local branch of the Women's Royal Voluntary Service (W.R.V.S.) will pay at least as much heed to the policy of headquarters as to the wishes of the local community. This in no way diminishes the value of the local W.R.V.S. as a contributor to the consideration of local problems, but if the W.R.V.S. member were on the community council by virtue of her membership of that organization rather than as an individual, she would be bound to feel accountable to the W.R.V.S. as well as to the community and if most of the members were similarly appointed conflicts would arise. Bryant[3] has pointed out that difficulties can occur if the organizational loyalties of members of a community (in his case, a tenants' association) inhibit them from behaving in ways preferred by the association's other members. Direct action may be sought by members whose only personal links are within the community itself but be resisted by those whose links with organizations or groups outside the area make them reluctant to jeopardize good relations in their affairs for the sake of making an effective protest relating to the locality alone. At this stage (which would last for the two years up to 1976 when the Act requires district councils to submit their schemes for community councils to the Secretary of State) there is a need for a central information centre whose role would be as follows:

1 To help local communities who asked for assistance to

find speakers or printed material on the subject,
2   To collect and disseminate information about experimental models and different forms of participation in Scotland and elsewhere (it would be necessary for the material to be carefully assessed, since the Scottish situation after the Act is distinctively different from any currently existing in U.K.),
3   To offer unbiased information, based on the best available knowledge, about the various options open to communities in forming local community councils and the likely consequences of any particular choice—financial, administrative, etc. For example, the Wheatley Report suggested that the local authority would provide the necessary secretrial support for the community councils in its area. If a community accepted this recommendation the results would almost certainly include
   a   close liaison between the community council and that part of the local authority whence the secretary came,
   b   closer links with the providing local authority (probably the district council) than with the regional council,
   c   some conflict of loyalty for the secretary between his employer and the community council,
   d   the possibility of difficulty if the community council wished to terminate the arrangement,
   e   subsidy in kind from the local authority. This might be regarded as an advantage by some community councils and a disadvantage by others.

A similar list could be compiled for the alternative of having a secretary drawn from the community itself. What is important here is that the local community should be able to evaluate for itself the likely consequences of the different choices. The office should not attempt to prescribe.

There is, therefore, a large job of education to be done *before* the district councils begin to prepare their schemes for community councils. How can the community hope to determine which size of area it feels to be best until it has had a chance to hold informed discussions upon the various issues involved in the choice? How can we ensure that the district councils take into account the vital importance of the links between community councils and the regional council unless we insist upon discussions about the proposed schemes with many bodies, including regional councils and Area Health Boards? A major weakness of the Wheatley Report's proposals is that although it speaks of the function of community councils *vis-à-vis* a variety of bodies, it presents the discussion of them as if they come in a natural order *below* the district councils which are themselves presented as *below* the regional councils. The vital point to grasp about community councils is that, although any one council may be concerned with a tiny area, it will be free to join with any number of others in a kaleidoscope of alliances, which will alter depending on the subject under discussion, and will often transcend district boundaries altogether.

That is the first great educational task which needs to be undertaken. The second should be a continuing one: the education of local communities and of councillors and officials in the localities about their areas and about the functions and structures of the bodies responsible for serving them. It is significant that S.N.A.P. found that one of the earliest initiatives taken by the inhabitants of Granby was to find out how the local authority worked[4] and Hilary Land has made a similar point about the expertise rapidly gained by claimants' unions on the operation of the Department of Health and Social Security. Much of this learning will take place only when an issue arises of sufficient concern to local residents to drive them into acquiring this information, but the new local authorities should become very much better prepared to explain their structures and methods of working than the former ones have been. There is no substitute for a teaching programme which is mainly staffed by those who are daily working in the authorities. I agree with the Skeffington report that local authority staffing should take account of this job and not leave it to the goodwill of busy officials to give an occasional lecture to a middle-class audience under the auspices of an adult educational programme. The aim here is not to have a continuous cycle of sparsely attended courses, but to produce (and keep up to date) attractive material on the operations of the authority so that when a community wishes to learn more about the processes of local government the officers will be able to draw upon good material.

Similarly, it will be necessary to produce information about the districts and community council areas within the region. It will often be salutary for the local authorities or the Area Health Boards to bring together groups of officials and members to discuss the problems of the region or district across the boundaries prescribed by the administrative machine. Study sessions for Health Service, regional and district council and central government officials and members, at which the future of the area as a whole could be discussed, should occur more often than at present. Attempts to predict the likely future patterns of tourism, traffic, employment, and housing based on the hardest available information should be discussed from a large number of different points of view. This sort of exercise should not be confined to a small number of senior officials but should be thrown open at regular intervals to the public. In Rousseau's democracy, the public would send members directly to participate in such 'courses' but in today's society it would be more realistic and effective to suggest that the community councils should make it part of their business to interest local people in such activities.

Time and expense are the two chief obstacles to the successful development of an educational/policy-making programme of this kind, but my suggestion has more to do with a shift in priorities than with the creation of an entirely new activity. Much of the reorganization of local government has been justified on the assumption that members will spend less time on detail and more on long-term planning than hitherto.[5] This may be unrealistic[6] but there is much to be said for making it easier for members to join with officials and interested members of the public in the sort of study of their area which at the moment is left to officials (mostly working within a single department) and to academics (busy within a single discipline). A farmer (or at least the National Farmers' Union) will often have as shrewd an idea of how an area will develop, as a housing specialist, and the young employee of an electronics factory may be able to contribute a forecast based on technological developments which could help to illuminate the discussion for all concerned. As schools increasingly teach 'civics' is it entirely fanciful to see the new education authorities keen to create increasingly sophisticated educational programmes for teaching citizens of every age about their own area at a level best suited to their interest and aptitudes?

I am conscious that such an approach reflects the bias of a professional educator, but there is discernible a growing hunger for practical education among voluntary organizations (see, for example the shift in direction of many large social welfare ones like Shelter or Christian Aid) towards education (propaganda, as some would assert) and even of the smaller ones like the National Council for One Parent Families who have just issued an information kit to help their clients and members. The educational conferences and courses of the unions and the political parties are increasing, both in number and in factual content, and anything which can be done to include in these curricula the study of local areas and to create the kind of joint sponsorship and consequent boundary crossing programme should be encouraged. Community councils might become admirable sponsors of such activities, backed with the educational resources of the local education authority, trades unions, local training boards, etc.

An increase in information certainly does not imply an increase in consensus and the use made of the material thus acquired will differ as much as the community differs in its views now. Indeed, it may even result in more conflict, since groups and individuals who are silent at present may acquire the confidence to make their views known, but the effort should result in a better-informed community and make it easier for it to exact accountability from its representatives and employees. It is meaningless to hope that the public will ever be able to monitor the performance of its policy makers without a considerably increased understanding of the goals and problems confronting them. It is similarly meaningless to hope for the maximum contribution from the public without up-to-date information. This, then, is the second great educational task confronting local government, for the main responsibility must rest upon it. The initiative might often come properly and effectively from the community councils, but the resources needed to mount such programmes regularly enough to be effective will have to be found chiefly by the regional or district authorities, although there is no reason why local unions, firms, voluntary organizations and individuals should not contribute to the costs.

Further Note on Material

Several of the appendices to the Skeffington Report contained suggestions about forms of exhibition, possible costs and ways of stimulating greater public interest. Since it was published there have been many more attempts at educational/involvement programmes and it is clear that there is already available a great deal of experience and expertise. Moreover, there is, equally, much experience in Europe and elsewhere about techniques and it would be desirable that there should be an information centre where all this could be gathered together. This might well prove to be a valuable second stage function of the national (or regional) information centre discussed above. A lending library of well-produced material illustrating principles and practices of general application could form the basis of many a local authority programme with much local material produced partly, no doubt, by community councils, simply to augment it. This centre would foster close links with bodies such as the airlines, British Rail, hotel chains, as well as local authorities, so that a wide variety of expertise and presentational opportunities would be available to it. The information exhibited about the Netherlands as a whole and about the Hague and Amsterdam in particular, in a foyer of the permanent conference centre in the Hague is a fine example of material which could provide a useful foundation for more localized exhibitions.

What is required is a political will to spend money upon this activity. The Hampshire County Council's evidence to the Skeffington Committee tried to work out the cost of the County Planning Department's normal work concerned with publicity for non-statutory plans. This is a continuous 'campaign' and is expressed as an annual cost. It covers attendance at public meetings, reading and evaluating letters of comment, meeting individuals and a good deal of correspondence. This is thought to take approximately five per cent of the working time of the particular staff concerned. After all this it comes as a surprise to learn that the bill to the department was assessed (a little low) at £1,570 per annum in 1966. If we continue to think that such sums are in some way good examples, we shall achieve very little in terms of community participation and the financial future of community councils looks black indeed. (See Chapter 4.)

The third educational task is even more subtle in some respects. The new councillors will require both instruction in their tasks and support in coping with the strains likely to result from increased participation. There are a number of major difficulties in the way of effective courses for councillors. The first is that it is always difficult to mount courses for prospective councillors except through the political parties. It would, for example, be difficult to persuade someone who was unlikely to win an election to attend a course. Yet if only those who expect to be successful attend, attendance will at once be taken as a sign of complacency and hugely increase the chance of a public pricking of the bubble. Moreover, before an election, candidates are fully occupied with electioneering. If the course is held afterwards, the new members are likely to be fully occupied with their new duties and, given a choice between a party-organized course, of the kind which is fairly common at present within the major parties, and one organized on the kind of non-party basis which a large-scale involvement of local authority officials and of community councils presupposes, most councillors would choose to learn about their party and its operations within the council.

There are thus mechanical problems about arranging a course. There are also psychological difficulties. Most experienced councillors are fairly sure that they understand better than anyone how to handle their constituents and would view as an impertinent irrelevance any suggestion that they require education in how to assist participation. Experience does not, however, endorse their belief. The obvious difficulties between S.N.A.P. and the local councillors are but one example of common problems. Active participation encourages hopes of effective action and when political or economic pressures outside the control of the local community defeat the participator's aims it is the elected representative who bears the brunt of their disappointment. The councillor needs both courage and patience to persevere with an activity which leads him into frequent bruising and the community needs to learn rapidly what are the constraints upon him. Increasingly, commerce and industry and the social services are learning that tensions of this sort can be understood and eased (though not, of course, eradicated) by sessions held by skilled interpreters of group activity who help both 'sides' to determine more clearly than before which are the tensions caused by differences of role and which are caused by genuine conflict of aim. Yet it would be unrealistic (even if it were desirable) to hold group sessions for the community council and their representatives unless there were also included some obvious and acceptable other function.

It would, therefore, seem sensible for a community council (or group of them) to mount a conference at which the public, the local officials and professionals and the local representatives could both teach each other about their locality and its place within the broader area and be helped, by sessions taken by someone with great expertise, to understand the various forces operating to create tensions between the community and their representative.

There is little likelihood of widespread acceptance of this suggestion, at least in the short term; nevertheless it would be fascinating if it were tried in a number of places and the results evaluated. I hope that the government or (failing that) some rich foundation will be prepared to invest a large sum of money to allow for experimentation of this sort in support of the new system and for its evaluation.

Notes

1. Craigmillar, Edinburgh, where the Festival Society has grown into a major community action and policy group.
2. Cramond, Edinburgh, where the residents' battle against the new runway at Turnhouse Airport drew at least some of its strength from existing groups.
3. R. Bryant, 'Play and Politics: A Case Study for Community Work' (*Social Work Today*, Vol. IV, No. 7).
4. 'In the meantime, the pioneer streets were already finding out the way local authorities worked: this was the real beginning of our participators' structure.' S.N.A.P. Report, 'Another Chance for Cities', p.61.
5. 'We believe, indeed, that the liberation of councillors from much routine decision-making will reduce the total time demanded of them and yet allow them more time for work in their constituencies.' Report and Royal Commission on Local Government in England S 506, Chapter XII.
6. See, for example, the estimate by the consultant local government review team that a regional councillor in Scotland will need to give twenty-six hours a week.

6

The Community Council in Practice

Almost everyone who has thought about community councils in Scotland (and similar bodies elsewhere in the United Kingdom) has confined their imaginings about them to a low level. This chapter argues that when we look at how the new councils might fit into our society new possibilities open up which would, if their challenge is accepted, reshape the whole of our democracy. If this seems an extravagant claim, let us look at our new animal as we have so far described it.

Every community in Scotland can have a community council of which every member of that community will have the right to be a member. In theory, at least, there will be no need to have standard boundaries nor a standard constitution, although in practice some uniformity of rule is likely to grow up. It would, for example, be impractical to give each individual member of the community the *right* to demand successfully that the community council convene a meeting on any particular subject. Some minimum number of signatories to such a demand could be required. If we are realistic we shall accept, moreover, that many areas will insist on a scheme which allows for an entirely traditional form of elected council despite all our experience that such bodies seldom work well for long. For the purpose of this chapter, however, I assume that many areas, if not all, do adopt a much less élitist form of organization on the lines discussed earlier.

We shall have, then, a mass of community councils in each district. No doubt most of them will spend most of their time discussing matters of direct relevance only to their own community, but they will also want to discuss many issues which range far wider than that. Area Health Board, transport or housing policy will often need to be discussed by groupings of community councils spread wide across large geographical areas. Indeed, in each district it is almost certain that a district association of community councils will grow up, if only to facilitate communications between the district council and its constituents. The same pressures are likely to have the same result at regional level and one can easily foresee the appearance of regional and district organizations to facilitate calling together appropriate groups from local community councils to discuss issues of regional or district significance. From here it is only a short step to a national association. This would, as in all the central office proposals outlined in my scheme, be small in permanent staff and its elected committee would, as at the local levels, have minimal duties. It would exist to convene and service meetings on issues which were of importance to all, or at least to large parts of the country, and to disseminate information.

Such meetings could be composed in a number of different ways including

1 Representatives directly elected by local community councils; the problem here would be the size of the gathering, which would be impossibly large except for meetings on very specialist or geographically limited issues,

2 Representatives elected by district associations of community councils. If each district in Scotland had an association and each association elected two representatives the total number would be 112,[1] which would be large but not entirely unworkable,

3 Delegates appointed by district associations. This would mean the same numbers as in 2 above but much tighter control over their activities than if they were representatives,

4 A mixture of delegates and representatives. This would allow for some of the likely differences between areas to be expressed and it would also be possible for some of the people sent to the national meetings to act as delegates on some issues and representatives on others.

It would, of course, also be possible for either the big meetings themselves or for any working groups established by them to co-opt or take evidence from people representing specific groups in the community. Thus it would be easy, for example, to obtain specialist advice from the trades unions (or from a specific group of trades unions), from employees, professional bodies and others. This would be in addition to any specialist advice which would come from individuals who took part in the discussions because they came from the community council network. After all, in a system in which people became involved because of their interest in a limited range of subjects there would already be a probability of much more specialized knowledge being available than in a system run for and by people with a general political interest. Indeed, not only might more specialist knowledge be available, it might be more readily offered if the possessor of it felt free to speak as a community council member rather than as a representative of some clearly defined group. The miner who attended because he lived in Dalkeith might be able to offer particularly valuable advice on some problem connected with the mining community, if he did not feel mandated by his local branch of the National Union of Mineworkers to represent its interests, in preference to those of the local community as a whole.

Whether at regional or at national level the new machinery could prove to be the most effective channel yet devised for enabling government to communicate with the governed. After all, as the Kilbrandon Commission reported, 'several witnesses suggested that the chief fault of government is its inability to communicate directly and simply with the people. One essential element which seems to be missing is a demonstrated willingness on the part of government to listen as well as to inform. Put simply, the contention is that government needs to do more to discover and understand the views and problems of ordinary people ...'[2] Community councils operating in the way I propose would make it hard indeed for government to excuse any similar failure in future. And not only government: the large industrial and commercial enterprises and many *ad hoc* agencies and other institutions would surely find a forum such as this, where they could both explain their policies and gather opinion upon it, invaluable both as an area of public relations and as a basis for acceptable policy making. The piecemeal, contumacious, expensive proceedings affecting oil developments in the North Sea might have been saved if a regional or national assembly of community councils had existed to discuss it with the oil companies, the government, the local authorities and other interested groups.

It is at this point, above all, that the relevance of these proposals extends out of Scotland to the U.K. as a whole. The Royal Commission on the Constitution, whether in the majority or minority report, argued for regional assemblies, not only for Scotland and Wales but also for the English regions. It is too early yet to say what will be the consequences of their reports although the appointment of Lord Crowther Hunt to advise the Government on the issues suggests that the minority proposals may carry the greater weight.[3]

The Royal Commission was concerned about the closeness of central control, the imposition of uniformity even where it was inappropriate, the lack of co-ordination within central government and the delays caused by over-centralization. It was also worried by the erosion of democracy which it saw in the growing power of the executive relative to the rest of the House of Commons and the growth of nominated or *ad hoc* bodies (of which there are already about fifty in Britain). They were also anxious about the secrecy of so much of our government, particularly that of the *ad hoc* bodies, whose operations are even less susceptible of public scrutiny than the elected authorities. Yet another worry was the inadequate provision for redress of individual grievances. For some of these problems the two reports suggested major changes in the structures of government. It may well be that administrative devolution to regional assemblies, whether or not they are charged with responsibilities for the *ad hoc* bodies within their region, will do something to improve matters. When we have had more experience of the new system of local government we shall be able to test the contention that more gifted and successful people would become representatives in the ordinary political way if there were a sufficiently satisfying job to be done at local level. It is possible that a regional tier of powerful government will go some way towards bridging the gap between the government and the governed although it seemed wide enough when there were 37,000 representatives for the population instead of the 24,000 now. Yet doubts inevitably remain. The majority report stated them clearly enough but shied away from providing any sort of solution: 'We ourselves have made no proposals, except by way of illustration.' Indeed, they contented themselves with mysticism.

It may be questioned whether a huge organization such as modern government, wielding great authority and with many diverse and unpopular tasks to perform, can possibly earn such trust in the eyes of the people or, except for strictly limited purposes, can expose itself to close and responsive contact with them. The most pertinent answer is that if these things are not possible we face a future in which government and people will grow further and further apart as the scope and complexity of government increases.[4]

Even if the proposals of the minority are accepted and a tier of regional governments is established which alone will have dealings with central government, the problem of 'us' and 'them' will undoubtedly persist. Neither group in the Royal Commission suggested that changes were required in the basic relationship between the elector and his representative. Whether or not technical changes in the method of election are introduced, the fact remains that the Royal Commission saw no need to change the basic principle that accountability to the electorate was secured by elections held at regular intervals. Moreover, there are no grounds whatsoever for imagining that the desirably high-powered, successful people who might flock to join a regional council will be less remote from their electors than the present councillors. The reverse is true. The councillor who prefers to deal with individual grievances and who is happiest when dealing with his constituents on the personal level is exactly the councillor whom the reorganization is designed to exclude. Reorganized local government is seeking high-class political managers who will feel at home in discussions about multi-million pound projects and whose principal concern with individual electors will be merely to spur on the officers to deal with them.

In such conditions the case for a new form of communication system is unanswerable and the community council is the best hope of building it. In Scotland the first brick has been laid in statute, but without real imagination among bureaucrats (at both central and local government level), elected members, voluntary organizations and the public itself, the chances to build higher will be missed and the opportunities deferred if not irretrievably lost. In England and Wales, as the present discussions indicate, there is a stage further still to go.

Objections

I turn now to some of the objections to the scheme. The following seem to be the most powerful:

1 The community council at whatever level it operates is only a 'talking shop' and no one will be interested,
2 It will be irresponsible,
3 It will confuse still further the public, which is already baffled by the complexity of government structures.

Let us take these in turn.

1 *It will be only a talking shop*

In his powerful note of dissent to the report of the Scottish Constitutional Committee and in subsequent elaborations, Professor Mitchell objected to the proposed Scottish Convention partly because, 'an examination of assemblies which can debate, but whose debate leads, and can only lead, to no positive outcome, compels a conclusion that such bodies inserted within the political machinery of government are unsatisfactory and injurious.'[5] Would this be true of a national, regional or local community council? There are good reasons for hoping not. In the first place, assemblies of the sort described by Mitchell nearly always have a semi-permanent membership and frequent (or at least regular) meetings. This at once implies that someone is busy collecting agenda whether or not there is any genuine desire to discuss the items. It also implies that the membership are expected to take an interest in a wide range of topics. In my scheme for community councils neither of these conditions would apply. Meetings would be held only if there were a demand for them and only those interested in the topics for discussion would usually attend. Thus instead of a structure which could be expected inexorably to bore the energetic and knowledgeable specialist or the enthusiastic or less knowledgeable layman out of attending the meetings at all, there would be a chance for them to come only to meetings which fired their imagination or kindled their wrath. Once again the majority report of the Constitution commission can be quoted: 'Some people who would not consider elective office might be prepared to serve in a more limited way.' The report went on to argue for more involvement of such people in consumer bodies and other similar groups, but it seems at least as likely that community councils would attract them when subjects close to them were up for discussion.

2 They might be irresponsible

This is a reasonable objection if we accept the conventional definition of irresponsible behaviour. This suggests that it is irresponsible to put forward ideas, policies, or criticisms if there is no likelihood of their proponent being asked to implement them or provide an alternative to the system under attack. Quite apart from the demonstrable fact that political parties behave like this frequently enough for the argument to have lost almost all its force, to argue this is to miss an important point about the proposed councils. They would be there to collect and make known the feelings as well as the intellectual positions of the community. As the Minority Report commenting on the attitude survey described it, 'The people are in fact at least as much concerned about "a felt lack of participation" as they are about a "felt lack of communication".' If people feel unreasonable it is valuable for government and its managers to know this early and it is foolish to dismiss 'unreasonable' explosions of feeling as valueless because 'irresponsible'. Moreover, the community council, at whatever level it is operating, will often provide for a 'brainstorming session' by all concerned and it is a common enough experience that some of the very best ideas have developed from widespread discussion of seemingly fantastic propositions.[6] It should also be remembered that community work experience argues against public irresponsibility in discussion meetings. It often happens that it is not the chairman or the professional or some other supposed repository of responsible standards who cuts unreasonable criticism or extravagant idealism down to size, but the other laymen present and many an uncomfortable meeting has ended in proposals radically different from those which the meeting started by discussing but which are nevertheless 'responsible'. Furthermore, it is often too easy for officials or elected members to be responsible, in the narrow sense of avoiding frivolous proposals or fecklessness in the expenditure of public money, but to be irresponsible in the sense of being too aloof from the consequences of their decisions really to care. Responsibility can imply being there to suffer the consequences of your own errors of judgement. Architects who never have to live in their blocks of flats or councillors who make policy for slums they will never visit are irresponsible in a sense which a local community meeting in council will seldom be.

3 *It will be confusing*

This is an argument loved by all political theorists and can be found amply used in the reports of both the Royal Commissions on Local Government and on the Constitution. Roughly speaking, the argument goes: 'The public already fail to vote in local government elections and studies show that only a small proportion of the electorate have any accurate understanding about the different levels of local government and their functions. If we add to the number of tiers or to the frequency of elections this confusion will grow worse and the apathy deepen.' Even if we accept this, it does not affect the position of the proposed community councils. The only direct elections involved in the scheme are those for the management group at the most local level. Since the functions proposed for that group are intended to be minimal a low turnout, or even an unopposed election (already so common in local government elections), matters very much less than it would in a system designed to select members of a ruling caucus secure from dismissal for three or four years. Thereafter, the council will function on the basic of public interest. If there is no interest the council will hardly function; if there is great interest there will be no difficulties about persuading people to participate in the selection of people to serve the community in relation to the particular topic currently exciting popular opinion.

A more likely and damaging source of confusion lies in the nature of the proposal itself. It seems certain that at first comparatively few people will feel secure in handling it and it will be difficult to prevent the community from seeking to return to the more conventional model. Even if a community decided to try it, there would be pressures towards the old system which might prove difficult to resist. For example, if a meeting of local residents decided to work towards a scheme for improving bad transport and produced a report for the local authority proposing that public funds should be used to subvent an experimental, semi-voluntary scheme of minibuses in the area, the local authorities might reasonably suggest that the local community become responsible for running the scheme itself. At this point the danger of confusion arises. It would be quite natural for members of the community to suggest that the community council take on the responsibility. It would be a mistake. What should be done would be for the community council to arrange for the community to establish a transport management group to run the scheme. This group would be accountable for the expenditure of public money and for the general running of the scheme and would thus behave like any voluntary organization. If complaint about the scheme became widespread the community council might well provide a forum for airing it; it would not itself run the scheme for it would have no continuing machinery for doing so. If it tried to acquire it, it would rapidly arrive at the position where its permanent staff and its management committee were so caught up in the day-to-day affairs of their executive duties that the opinion collecting, information disseminating function would suffer in consequence.

A further advantage of the separation of the executive and deliberative functions lies in the likely reduction of the monopoly position of the political parties. A system designed to crystallize and make known the different strands of public opinion will be much less subject to party domination. Nothing can or should be done to prevent political activists from taking part in the deliberations of the community councils, but there is nothing in their proposed operation to make the party labels an essential or even appropriate feature. Just as the Conservatively inclined district of Cramond became the most active opponents of a government policy under the last Conservative government, so community councils at every level will be full of people wishing to make their views clearly known on a wide variety of issues without paying heed to their wider party allegiances. Give the community councils executive functions and budgets and the political pressures to bring them under party control will prove irresistible and we shall rapidly return to the present sterile political debate which seems to be such an important factor in public apathy.

If, then, we can accept that some of the most likely objections to the scheme are answerable, how well does it cope with the anxieties expressed by the Royal Commission on the Constitution? On *closeness of central control* it has little to contribute since this is mainly a matter of legislative and financial domination, but if there were a network of lively, well-informed assemblies at every level in a region, it would be harder for central government to argue that it needed to retain close control in order to protect the public from local authorities' incompetence or sluggishness. Still less would central government be able to insist on *uniformity*, whether appropriate to local circumstances or not. Apologists for the present insistence on uniform standards of provision claim that even if at times it is excessive, this is only because central government extrapolates known demands for uniformity in some fields (like schools provision) into others (like housing) because there is no reliable way of testing local public feeling. With effective community councils that lack would be made good and a much clearer idea of public preferences would in time emerge.

On the *lack of co-ordination* in central government the system would probably have only one effect. Regular contact with lay opinion at every level would strengthen the pressures for greater co-ordination at every level of government. The community councils will bring together the public both as consumers and as providers. In particular, over issues which span several departmental interests or fall across authorities of different type or level, the difficulties caused by inadequate co-ordination would be highlighted and the pressure to eradicate them grow rapidly.

The question of *delay* is more difficult. We have already glanced at the problem in Chapter 1 and it seems likely that greater public participation will slow down the earlier stages of policy making but speed up the later, more expensive ones. The creation of articulate, well-informed public groups is likely to bring pressure on the bureaucracy to reduce delays which are unavoidable but may, on the other hand, increase certain work-loads by demanding to be kept better informed.[7]

The *erosion of democracy* should be slowed down, if not reversed, for a number of reasons. In the first place, the elected representatives at both local and central government level should be able to command a very much more effective research and information machine than they have ever had before. This will go some way towards diminishing the ill-effects of having to spend more time on parliamentary or local government business. Second, the system would give many more people an opportunity to take a meaningful part in the making of policy in our society. By so doing, it would greatly increase public understanding of the whole democratic system. Moreover, it might make possible the sort of distinction between managerial and consumer protection functions which the Maud report so glibly assumed would follow from an administrative reorganization of local government. Third, the involvement of many more people at every level should go some way towards reducing the *secrecy* in which so much business is currently transacted. A community councils' association at district level might well concern itself with its elected members' rules governing the conduct of council business and often it is enough to ask the question 'why?' to reveal the absurdity of many of them. A lively association would seem at first threatening to many councillors, but as it became clear that they were challenging the structure as much as the individuals in it, they would often be recognized as allies against all those tacit assumptions which are the principal reason why machines of government eventually control all who work within them.

Another problem in which the community councils would be helpful is that of *controlling the* ad hoc *bodies* which proliferate with such unnerving speed. Even if many of them remain necessary, their operation would be unlikely to escape scrutiny if there were an effective community council system to collect public feeling about them and pass it on. It might be that, at least in the short term, the various specialist groups which already try to represent the consumer interest should remain in being but if there were behind them a community council to serve as a forum for discussing their affairs a number of

advantages would accrue. First, the present separateness of
their operations could be questioned. It is, as always, in the
community itself that the relationships between the various
bodies become most apparent and the impact of the Post Office
Giro upon the billing policy of the Gas and Electricity Boards
or the unequal impact of higher postal charges imposed without
consideration of the number of public telephone boxes available
within a community can be thrashed out. Again, it is probable
that in many of the debates in the community council comments
which reflect upon the operations of the *ad hoc* bodies will be
made and, if collected together over a period, would provide
valuable evidence of how their policies work out in practice.
It has never been a particularly valid point to make that if
the number of written complaints received is low the level of
public satisfaction is high. Many bad policies result in many
people suffering needlessly and someone who has had to wait
six months for some maintenance operation to be carried out
may well not complain to any consumer body, unaware of five
hundred other people in the same predicament. Yet a community council meeting called to discuss local amenities might
produce overwhelming evidence of dissatisfaction about electricity maintenance or the inadequacy of transport to the local
hospital.

A third aspect of greater control for *ad hoc* bodies relates
to the selection of people to sit on them. At the moment, one
of the most striking features of our society is the poverty of
imagination displayed in the appointment of people to public
bodies. In most instances, an important role is played by the
civil service and it has been truly said that, 'there are few
sights in Britain more pathetic than that of an assistant secretary
looking for a new nominee to submit to a minister for a public
appointment'. The reason is that the machinery for discovering
such people is woefully inadequate. Political parties, local
authority and other major association officials, ministers themselves and the civil service are, by their nature, likely to throw
up names drawn from a depressingly narrow swathe of society.
Bureaucrats newly retired, academics, public figures over-
occupied with professional or voluntary activities, representative
councillors (known to central government and therefore likely
to be more burdened than the rest) predominate and, of course,

their average age is far too high. How different the picture would look if there were a network of public gatherings which could be consulted. The very nature of the community councils' proceedings makes it easier to find suitable people since most of their meetings would be based on particular topics. It would, therefore, be much easier than it usually is to evaluate the likely contribution of an individual to a particular body. At present, too many are chosen on an ill-defined belief that because they are public-spirited and reasonably well known they will have a special contribution to make to the Gas Council. If community councils were asked to submit names for public bodies at both regional and national level the chances of widening the charmed circle of the establishment would be greatly increased.

Finally, *redress of grievances*. The Royal Commission was understandably anxious about this and the rapid growth in Citizens' Advice Bureaux and in consumer rights' organizations both indicate wide public anxiety also. It would probably be an unjustifiable extension of the community council's operations to expect it to take up individual cases of bad treatment. Yet, as we have seen, the council's meetings are likely to throw up many instances of dissatisfaction, which would prove valuable in any attempt to alter the general policy of a department or agency. Moreover, it would often be of enormous value to the various agencies working on behalf of individuals if there were available an independent body ranging much more widely than themselves to add weight to their plea for an enquiry or for public support. In some areas one could imagine that the consumer rights' organizations might join together to form a working group which would, from time to time, seek a meeting convened by the community council to give wider coverage to its labours. Moreover, if it appeared that a particular public agency was so much in need of reform that little short of a change of management would do, the community council's aid in collecting widespread evidence of dissatisfaction would clearly be indispensable.

There is, then, in the terms of the Royal Commission on the Constitution, a strong argument for introducing a system of community councils, not only in Scotland where some kind of new system is inescapable, but throughout the United Kingdom. As the reports pointed out, dissatisfaction with our present structures is as harshly felt in England as in Scotland or Wales and if a solution looks good for one of the latter why should the rest be denied its benefits?

Notes

1. Including the island regions as districts.
2. Majority report, paragraph 317.
3. The recent publication by the Government of their discussion paper, 'Devolution within the U.K.' (H.M.S.O. 1974), draws upon both reports.
4. Majority report, paragraph 1245.
5. Note of Dissent. Report of Scottish Constitutional Committee, 1970. Paragraph 5.
6. 'In my course I have known and, according to my measure, have co-operated with great men; and I have never yet seen any plan which has not been mended by the observations of those who were much inferior in understanding to the person who took the lead in the business.' Edmund Burke quoted in K. Popper, *The Open Society and its Enemies*. Routledge and Kegan Paul 1973.
7. cp. Marris and Rein, *Dilemmas of Social Reform*, 2nd edn. Routledge and Kegan Paul 1972.

7
Implications
for the Rest of the U.K.

So far I have related much of what I have said to Scotland, because there the Government has a statutory obligation to oversee a national system for obtaining community participation. Yet there is no reason why most of what I have suggested for Scotland should not be considered also for England and Wales. Indeed, there are already proposals for legislation to establish local councils in urban areas, roughly similar to the parish or community councils so familiar in the rural areas. This chapter is, therefore, a plea to the government, and all others interested in participation, to think more boldly than they have hitherto and to give serious consideration to a system much more far-reaching than anything so far considered.

Let me start with a brief description of some of the major features of the English and Welsh scene. Perhaps the biggest single difference between the Scottish situation and that south of the Border lies in the continued statutory existence of parish councils. In England the rural parish remains as 'the parish' and former urban districts and boroughs also become parishes, sometimes called 'successor parishes'. The district councils have to establish these according to the provisions of the Local Government Act 1972 and detailed sections are included in the Act governing elections, meetings, the position of the chairman, the taking of minutes and much else.[1] In Wales the name 'parish' has been superseded by the name 'community', but in most respects the new communities resemble very closely the old parishes. Rural parishes were given the automatic right to continue as new communities, and their councils as community councils but, in addition, those urban districts and boroughs which wished to do so could apply to their district councils for community council status and ninety did so. In both England and Wales it is laid down that only local government electors can be voting members of these councils and in every way it is made clear that the new councils are expected to be, like their predecessors, modelled upon the traditional pattern of democracy questioned throughout this book. It is indeed laid down that community councillors should serve for four years, so that even the sanction of an election can only be threatened at long intervals.

The reasons for this persistence of the former tradition are clear enough and can perhaps be seen most effectively set out in the evidence to the Royal Commission on Local Government from the National Association of Parish Councils (now renamed the National Association of Local Councils). This was succinct, cogent and particularly persuasive because it rested on the experience of 6,200 member councils.

What were the principal features of this evidence? First, the Association was essentially conservative. It saw no reason to alter the traditional electoral arrangements, which were based on the electoral roll and which, on average, resulted in a council rather closer to the electorate as a whole in age and composition than the local elections for larger councils.

Second, it found no fault with the financial system, which gave parish councils the right to precept upon the rates, although it would have liked better access to inexpensive capital. Third, it clearly saw the councils as responsible for running services at their own hand and saw any change in this in terms merely of the councils being given a chance to do more. Any suggestion that the deliberative and the executive functions might be split was firmly ruled out. It is important the Association claimed that the representatives of grassroots democracy should have something to do as well as to say and that they should, have real, if local, power because nothing else would ensure a responsible attitude to public affairs.

This is a clear statement of the traditional view and commands respect because parish councils have achieved a remarkable improvement in their position in local government in recent years. Moreover, a great part of that improvement can be attributed to the indefatigable efforts of two men whose influence on the evidence can hardly be doubted: Charles Arnold-Baker, the Secretary of the National Association of Local Councils, and Professor Keith-Lucas.

Among the successes won by the Association were a widening of the functions which could be discharged by the parish (or, in Wales, community) council and of the powers to undertake them. Thus, the Act abolished the old limitations on expenditure known as the rate limitations but retained, in England, the old 'free two pence'—the product of a two penny rate which can be spent without reference to the local authority. The Act did not abolish the *ultra vires* principle and the functions of local councils remain prescribed, although widened. Yet a look at what these are reveals the disadvantages of insisting upon a traditional 'lowest level' tier of local government. Car parks, footpaths, seats and bus shelters, public lavatories, litter bins, washhouses and allotments, village halls and local bands; these are much of the fare on the daily menu of most local councils under the Local Government Act. Nobody who has lived in a rural area, particularly, would underestimate the importance of all these in creating and maintaining a comfortable, convenient and civilized life for the community. Many parish councils can point with pride to a strengthening of local bonds and a marked improvement in the quality of local life thanks to their watchful care of such provision. Moreover the valuable powers to indemnify the post office or a transport contractor against losses incurred on local services provide a means of keeping a local community alive.

In addition, one major victory was secured in the field of planning. Under the Local Government Act, Schedule 16, paragraph 20, the district council *is bound* to send a local council particulars of any planning applications concerning land in its area. Moreover, the district council is required to take into account any comments which the local council may make within fourteen days of the notification (and may consider further comments made later). Fourteen days is not enough to secure full consideration by any but the local councillors themselves, but it is an obligation on the district council which should be improved and copied in Scotland also.

Yet when all is said and done, the parish or community council in England and Wales remains unmistakably the bottom level of local government. It is confined to consideration or performance of the cheaper parts of public expenditure. It is undoubtedly valuable and important for local people to be informed of, and even able to control, minor developments of purely local importance, and there is a noticeable dearth of devices for achieving this. But if our major structure for involving local people is confined to this, their influence on the forces which shape the society in which they live will remain peripheral. How a local community fills the space underneath the arches of a motorway flyover is certainly important, but it is very secondary to the importance of having a chance to influence motorway policy itself. If, however, the executive and deliberative functions remain linked and the traditional method of electing an élite for a long period remains the only way to obtain a local council, there is no likelihood of the latter obtaining significantly more influence over the policy makers. After all, what arguments are there to persuade one élite, composed of people who have (at least in theory) campaigned on their suitability to make a policy on a fairly large scale, to share this valued power with another élite which has been elected on a much more local platform?

It is not surprising that the Association of Parish Councils takes such a conservative view. They are based mainly in rural areas and they were concerned to win as many concessions as possible in the short term from traditionally minded politicians, and the Association itself is made up of those members of the local élite who have derived most satisfaction from the present structure. What is very much more alarming is that the present campaign to extend statutory local councils into the urban areas seems to be proposing little more than a copy of the rural system.

The most vigorous body in the campaign is the Association of Neighbourhood Councils, whose secretary is Bob Dixey, a councillor from Essex. The founder of the Association was Michael Young of the Institute of Community Studies and, significantly enough, a leading founder member of it was Mr Arnold-Baker (secretary of the National Association of Local Councils). The aim is to create a national system of neighbourhood councils within the town and urban agglomerations omitted from the local councils system under the Local Government Act 1972. Its hope is to obtain legislation eventually so as to win for the neighbourhood councils a statutory status equal to that of the parish councils. In the meantime it works to establish non-statutory councils as prototypes suitable for assimilation to the new structure. Partly because of the advantages of a uniform model when legislation is being prepared and partly, no doubt, because of a belief in the dangers of 'irresponsibility' if the rules are left to local discretion, the association is trying to promote a model constitution. This is based on that used for the election of the Grove Park community council in Hammersmith. This presents a conventional scheme: first, define the area or neighbourhood; second, hold elections based on an agreed formula for determining the ratio of councillors to electors. Those elected will hold power for a predetermined period. The electorate should consist of those on the electoral roll and would, therefore, exclude young people, newly arrived residents and some other groups, although there is some talk of a supplementary register to reduce this problem.

Because one of the strongest arguments against increasing public participation has been low turnout at elections, the Association stresses the value of making the elections truly democratic. They hope to achieve this by building into the system a number of techniques designed both to assist even the poorest representatives of minorities to stand for election, and to increase the number of people casting their votes. They have proposed, for example, that there should be only one election address carrying the photographs and manifestos of all the candidates. This would be delivered by volunteers to every house and the ballot box might similarly be taken from door to door. It is clear, therefore, that the Association is genuinely anxious to secure an even greater degree of public participation than exists in many rural areas and it is, perhaps, no surprise to learn that it has received considerable all-party support, at least in principle. Yet there are good reasons for viewing the scheme doubtfully. In the first place, even the best known prototype election, that of Golborn Neighbourhood Council, produced a disappointing poll. It was a good deal higher than the poll for the borough council election but was still under fifty per cent. The election did secure a number of energetic, committed local people (and some equally committed from outside) to fight for the improvement of the neighbourhood and several worthwhile victories were won. Yet its life was dogged by conflicts which seem to have arisen as much between the elected members as between interest groups within the community itself. When the original council collapsed the newsletter *Community Action* commented

> Although the Golborn Neighbourhood Council has accomplished many things, there is little doubt that it has been constrained by its formal structure ... it will be necessary to look outside conventional democracy to find a framework more suitable to community action. It may be desirable to incorporate local action and pressure groups within the neighbourhood council; make the council accountable to regular public meetings; or develop a system of street groups to which the council would be responsible.

In other words, one answer to the weaknesses of the traditional model is not, as the Association of Neighbourhood Councils sometimes seem to be suggesting, to make the rules against manipulation of the electoral system tighter, but rather to loosen the whole system up. The vital need is to ensure direct accountability to the public at large and this can best be secured by direct and frequent contact with the public. It is not because people elected in the traditional way, and thus largely secured for a period against directly expressed public disapproval, grow necessarily corrupt nor inefficient; it is simply that the nature of their work and of the system in which they do it makes it difficult for them to keep in close enough touch with the changing moods of the community, especially of those sections which did *not* elect them.

As for the problem of a low poll, the only answer the proponents of the traditional model can suggest is to intensify the campaign to sell a product to which the people are demonstrably indifferent. For them to be satisfied, the elections would have to have regularly, over a long period, a very high turnout at the polls. There is no reason to expect any such outcome. The combination of inadequate safeguards for the different minorities within the community and the difficulty of stimulating enough interest in a widely varied electoral platform will ensure low polls in most neighbourhoods most of the time.

Another problem of the proposed model lies in the position of the political parties within it. In systems designed primarily or exclusively to put forward opinions, conventional party loyalties need not be paramount. In systems designed to perform executive duties they are likely to be so. This danger is made even more threatening by the fact that the A.N.C. is rolling its bandwaggon by frightening the political parties. It suggests that if they do not organize themselves at the neighbourhood council level their opponents will.[2] Indeed, some of the A.N.C. leaders are quite explicit about the possible party advantages to be derived from such involvement. This is not to suggest that the A.N.C. advocates party alignments in the neighbourhood councils, quite the reverse. They are insistent that people should not stand for election under a national party label. The trouble is that under their model it is hard to see how they can reconcile a number of conflicts. If the neighbourhood councils are to have significant sums of money to spend and important executive functions to perform, the political parties will want to be directly involved. If their members are expected to take an interest in every issue which affects the neighbourhood it will often be in the ranks of the local politicians that such polymaths must be sought. A third problem is that if under such a system political affiliations do emerge, co-operative action between neighbour- hood councils on issues affecting a wide area will be more difficult. Under an issue-based system Tory, Liberal and Labour neighbourhoods might find it quite easy to discover common opinions on a particular issue affecting them all because the people concerned in creating that opinion would not have explicit party links. In a traditional system the party links are likely to obtrude to the detriment of a common front. If the party affilia- tions become important at the neighbourhood level a further difficulty would be the tendency to support a candidate because of his label rather than because of his suitability as an individual.

It is true that parish councils have largely succeeded in avoiding party labels. We cannot know whether this is because the majority of the issues with which they deal are minor ones, or because the idea of independent politics lived longest in rural areas. Perhaps the same would occur in the urban areas, but it seems more likely that it will be the major political parties, often represented by people who have lost their present oppor- tunity to serve on the council, who will take the lead in creating the new neighbourhood councils. If they do, it will not only be in the form with which they are already familiar, but with definite links to the political organizations of which they are members. This danger would be much more easily avoided if the personnel directly involved in discussing a particular problem changed as the problem changed. If, in addition, the council really acted as a channel of communication for the neighbourhood and allowed contributions by any member, or group of members, to go forward, there would be little incentive to create a permanent majority. The A.N.C. model may be a reasonably satisfactory one for the running of services; it is very disappointing as a channel of community opinion.

It would be particularly sad if the widespread adoption of the A.N.C. model, or even its creation by statute, began to throttle the richly diverse growth of neighbourhood experiments all over the United Kingdom.

At present, there seem to be at least three main strands of development. The first, and most institutional, is the coming together of established voluntary organizations in new groupings to match the reorganized local authorities. This is an adaptation of the existing council of social service pattern and will clearly lead to a number of headaches, but will no doubt gradually result in a new national network of councils of social service, looking more or less directly to the National Councils of Social Service for central services. The most obvious problems can be seen in Scotland and in the Metropolitan districts of England. In the former a working party of the Scottish Council of Social Service under Miss Margaret Herbison has recommended the establishment of new regional groupings of voluntary organizations to make communication between them and the new local authorities easier. The group points out that some arrangements will need to be made to ensure adequate coverage of issues at the district level also. In the Metropolitan counties a similar problem has been recognized and a project team financed by two trusts has been looking at possible solutions. Based on its reports, the National Council of Social Service and the central government have been proposing that community development workers be paid to help those districts, which have not yet got councils of social service, to establish them and to create thereafter adequate regional machinery to cope with the issues best handled at that level. Similar developments are being worked out in other areas. There are problems of inter area jealousies, of personalities and of deep-seated anxieties lest some consortium of voluntary bodies in a large conurbation should attempt to dominate the rural organizations. Yet experience suggests such fears are usually exaggerated and that machinery for effective co-operation can be devised. Here, too, the more the central body can steer clear of executive responsibilities the better. The moment that it appears as a direct competitor with one of its own members in a field of work in which differences of opinion are anyway common, its position as an impartial co-ordinator is undermined.

If an effective national network of metropolitan, district and county organizations can be established to supply information to and collect it from the voluntary bodies, the value of them to our society will be increased. Yet valuable though this will be, it is distinct from the other two strands. These are local councils and community action. We have already discussed the former, but it is worth stressing that, particularly within the towns and cities, a diversity of pattern is growing up. In some places the local authorities have themselves taken the lead in creating neighbourhood councils. Lambeth, for example, has established eight of them.

> The concept was quite different from that of the statutory 'urban parishes' advocated by the A.N.C., National Association of Local Councils and the Liberal Party. Lambeth's neighbourhood councils existed, initially at least, by courtesy of the borough council. They would represent 'activists' of local communities, not the will of the whole community as expressed through the ballot box.[3]

Incidentally, they were funded at £22,000 per annum or 5p. per head—a sum worth remembering when we think about finance for participation. Freeman goes on to suggest that one of the weaknesses of a local authority model is that they can be 'dismissed, or ignored as not democratically representative of the community ...'. A different sort of initiative has been taken by Liverpool, where the new Liberal-controlled council has given very senior officer status to the chief community development officer, with the result that a large number of local initiatives can be helped and supplied with information from a high level within the council itself.

In other places local amenity groups have progressed into the provision of social services or into participating with the local and other authorities in policy discussions. In some areas housing co-operatives, tenants' associations, community arts groups, claimants' unions, playgroups and many others have found themselves combining their original functions with new ones. Sometimes one feels that the local authority has come reluctantly to consult such groups because they are afraid of them. Sometimes it seems as if the local authority has seized upon them eagerly, at least at first, as a way of satisfying themselves that they have genuinely mounted the participation/ consultation bandwaggon. These kinds of local groups may be from rich or poor areas and all of them tend to run into the same difficulties over the legitimacy of their position. When conflict breaks out, either between the local authority and the groups, or between different factions within them, it is easy to deny that they have the right to speak for the area.

The same difficulty afflicts the groups woven into our third strand: community action. Yet these tend, as Robert Holman has pointed out, 'to arise in areas of high need and to concentrate on specific issues'.[4] Thus Battersea Redevelopment Action Group have been locked in a battle over the council's proposed large-scale redevelopment scheme. Rainthorpe Residents' Association in Yorkshire has formed to protect local interests against a new landlord of a majority of houses in the village. The dividing line between local councils and community action is hard to define, particularly in areas where any local council would draw all or most of its constituency from the same group as a community action group. Yet what is important is that most of these new community action groups receive their vigour from issues which stir large numbers of local people, rather than from some form of institutionalized imitation of parliamentary democracy. In the short term, at least, it is unreal to expect devolution of large-scale power to very local groups. Arnold-Baker has, indeed, questioned whether it would ever be welcome.

In running a refuse collection service or a lighting system democracy seems hardly relevant: it is expertise and system which matter. It is arguable that if the public indulges in democratic interference something is bound to go wrong. It is, in any event, certain that the public does not want to know. It will complain, of course, if things go astray, and this is fair enough because it pays, but if I buy a washing machine which goes wrong I want another washing machine for my money, not a change in the board of directors. Participation works in some places and not others.[5]

His argument can be assailed at many points. For example, if the directors of the company will not replace a faulty washing machine there is a good deal to be said for insisting on directors who will. More important, a community might very well prefer a chance to influence refuse collection policy to tame acquiescence in someone else's idea of what the policy should be. A refuse collection service based on density of population per acre might be infinitely more attractive to a community than one based on two collections per week regardless of area. Yet it remains true that the public is never likely to be consistently interested in the technicalities of service provision and it is most improbable that those who are will try to make them show more interest. What matters is that we should establish a system sufficiently strong financially, broadly enough based and flexible enough in its structure to ensure that when policy is first being considered the views of local communities are taken into account. We are extraordinarily feeble in our application of this dogma. Has anyone ever tried to ask a local community how it would spend £20 million if it had the choice? I doubt it. Yet redevelopment plans for such sums are always being dreamed up in offices remote from the redevelopment area itself. How many local communities, given compulsory purchase powers and vast sums of money to spend, would produce a priority list which resembled that of the planners? If we took pains to help local groups work out various policy options from the beginning we might find that between their ideas and those of the bureaucrats and speculators a compromise could be achieved which would satisfy more aspirations than either would manage on their own. If we create a participatory system confined to minor functions and, in practice at least, built on a minority base we shall throw away an opportunity for boldness and condemn ourselves and those of our children who care about democracy to a labour of Sisyphus. We shall be asking them to pick down the pyramids with a pin. By all means set up local bodies to administer local playgrounds, but let us also have local councils for contributing to the making and monitoring of policy, which are elastic enough to cope with the largest as well as the smallest scale. This is the challenge before British democracy. If we meet it, who can foresee what will result? In the surge of self-confidence which would follow upon a genuine trusting of the 'ordinary public' all sorts of institutions—schools, industry, local government and parliament itself—might be revitalized. If we do not, disillusion will breed either violence or apathy and we shall deserve our subsequent distress.

Notes

1. Local Government Act 1972, sections 9-17.
2. 'If the Labour Party does not get on and do it, either from Opposition or once it is in Government, then we shall find ourselves being forced to take an interest from behind. The councils are only just beginning and I should like to see the Labour Party give them a lead.' Bob Dixey in *Labour Weekly* 24 August 1973.
3. Freeman, *Municipal and Public Services Journal*, 21 September 1973.
4. R. Holman, 'Why Community Action?' (*Municipal and Public Services Journal*, 5 April 1973).
5. 'A Ray of Hope' (*Local Government Chronicle*, 29 March 1974).

Appendix

Note: These figures are based on the best obtainable 'guesti-mates'. They have been extracted from Rate Support Grant and Local Financial Return Statements of the out-turn by local authorities for the year 1971-2, as apportioned and aggregated to match the new region and islands areas. They relate to 'reckonable' expenditure only (that is, expenditure met from rates and government grants on rating services, including housing). They exclude revenue-producing undertakings. Where a return of an existing authority is relevant to more than one region, island, or district, the content has been apportioned between areas by simple reference to population falling into the new regions, islands area and districts. This may lead to errors.

Table

One per cent of revenue expenditure met from rates and government grants by new regions, compiled from 1971-2 R.S.G./L.F.R. returns.

	Region	£
1	Highland	201,640
2	Grampian	426,030
3	Tayside	389,610
4	Fife	311,650
5	Lothian	729,440
6	Central	285,910
7	Borders	95,620
8	Strathclyde	2,831,470
9	Dumfries and Galloway	127,990
10	Orkney	19,520
11	Shetland	20,860
12	Western Isles	38,140

Bibliography

Area 44 Health Services' Project, 'The Consumer and The Health Service', Report by Second Phase Advisory Group.

Arnold-Baker, Charles, 'A Ray of Hope' (*Local Government Chronicle*, 29 March 1974).

Beveridge, Lord, *Voluntary Action*. Allen and Unwin 1949.

Bryant, R., 'Play and Politics: A Case Study for Community Work' (*Social Work Today*, Vol. IV, No. 7).

Bulpitt, J. G., 'Participation and Local Government: Territorial Democracy' in G. Parry, ed., *Participation in Politics*. Manchester University Press 1972.

Castle, Barbara, National Health Service Bill, *Hansard*, Vol. 842, Col. 350, 1 August 1972.

'Community Councils', Scottish Development Department Circular, L/LGR/48, 1972.

Constitution, Royal Commission on the, H.M.S.O. 1973, Cmnd 5460.

'Devolution Within the United Kingdom', H.M.S.O. 1974.

District Councils Association, Circular No. 1972/39.

Donnison, D., 'The Micro-Politics of the Inner City'.

Focus Magazine.

Freeman, L., 'Third Tier Urban Government' (*Municipal and Public Services Journal*, 21 September 1973).

French, J. R. P., Israel, J., and Aas, D., 'An Experiment in Participation in a Norwegian Factory' (*Human Relations*, Vol. XIII, No. 1, 1960).

Harrison, P., 'The Neighbourhood Council' (*New Society*, 12 April 1973).

Hatch, S., ed., *Towards Participation in Local Services*, Fabian Tract, No. 419.

Holman, R., 'Why Community Action?' (*Municipal and Public Services Journal*, 5 April 1973).

Kavanagh, D., 'Political Behaviour and Participation', in Parry, G., ed., *Participation in Politics*. Manchester University Press 1972.

Local Government Act, 1972.
Local Government (Scotland) Act, 1973.
Local Government (Scotland) Bill, First Scottish Standing Committee, *Hansard*, Cols. 1525 and 1545, 10 April 1973.
'Local Government in England', Report of Royal Commission, H.M.S.O.
'Local Government in Scotland', Report of Royal Commission, 1966-9, Cmnd 4150, H.M.S.O. 1969.

Management of Local Government, Report of the Committee on, H.M.S.O.
Marris, P., and Rein, M., *Dilemmas of Social Reform*. Routledge and Kegan Paul 1972.

National Health Service (Scotland) Bill, *Hansard*, 13 June 1972.

Parry, G., ed., 'Political Behaviour and Participation' in *Participation in Politics*. Manchester University Press 1972.
Pateman, C., *Participation and Democratic Theory*. C.U.P. 1970.
Popper, K., *The Open Society and Its Enemies*. Routledge and Kegan Paul 1973.
'Public Participation in Planning'. Ministry of Housing & Local Government, Scottish Development Department, and Welsh Office, 1969.

Rousseau, J. J., *The Social Contract*. O.U.P. 1971
Rowe, A., 'Community Councils', Scottish Council of Social Service, Occasional Paper No. 1, 1973.

'Scotland's Government', Scottish Constitutional Committee Report, 1970.
Select Committee on Nationalized Industries.
Shelter Neighbourhood Action Project Report, 'Another Chance for Cities', 1972.

Skeffington Report, see 'Public Participation in Planning', above.
Social Work (Scotland) Act, 1968.

Townsend, P., *The Last Refuge*. Routledge and Kegan Paul 1964.

Verba, S., *Small Groups and Political Behaviour*. Princeton University Press 1961.

Index